For Ken Burns

Tom & Virginia of Swans Island

To Virginia

*A*velinda

The Legacy of a Yankee Yachtsman

THOMAS D. CABOT

Island Institute, Rockland, Maine

Published by:
Island Institute
P.O. Box 429
Rockland, Maine 04841

Distributed by:
Tilbury House, Publishers
132 Water Street
Gardiner, Maine 04345

Cover and text designed on Crummett Mountain by Edith Allard.
Layout: Mark Melnicove.
Imagesetting: High Resolution, Inc., Camden, Maine.
Printing: Arcata Graphics, Halliday, West Hanover, Massachusetts (text and binding); Western Maine Graphics, Norway, Maine (cover, dustjacket and color folio).

Library of Congress Number: 91-75009

10 9 8 7 6 5 4 3 2

Contents

ACKNOWLEDGEMENTS

Many people had a hand in bringing this book together. Thanks are due to the editorial team—Philip Conkling, Brenda Gilchrist, and Cynthia Bourgeault—who helped shape and amplify the manuscript, and to the writers who contributed sidebars on various aspects of island life: Philip Conkling on Cross and Butter islands, Cynthia Bourgeault on Swans Island, George Putz on the Gamage shipyard, and Robert Kimber on the Maine Coast Heritage Trust (this essay, in an expanded version, originally appeared in Down East *magazine, January 1991.)*

Thanks are due as well to Peter Ralston, who selected the photographs from the Cabot family's extensive collection and wrote the introduction to the color folio section; to Mary Mohler and Robert Hylander, who furnished additional images of Swans Island; and to David Willauer, who provided the map of Cross Island. And special thanks go to Edith Allard, who supervised the design and layout of the book and managed the production timetable with a firm yet gentle hand.

Introduction

You Have To Look Ahead Into The Future To Get The Full Measure Of appreciation from Tom Cabot's recollections of *Avelinda,* which cover nearly a century of observation, insight, and concern over what the Maine coast represents in American life. In the twenty-first century, people who read about Tom Cabot's life will find it difficult to believe that one individual could be credited with so many distinctive achievements within a single lifetime.

If Tom Cabot were known only for having engineered and presided over a very successful international corporation which turns natural gas into a diversified array of products from carbon black to useable energy, his name would be assured a place in American history as an innovative industrialist. But like Tom Cabot, other American industrialists also tempered their careers with stints serving the country in government posts. It is also true that other such men have been drawn to the sea for respite, refreshment, and recreation, because sailing vessels are, after all complicated craft which require nerve, purpose, and clarity, not unlike the skills necessary for navigating corporate enterprise through the straits of Scylla and Charybdris.

Here on the Maine coast, Tom Cabot, along with extraordinary shipmates—among others, Alexander Forbes, Charles Francis Adams, and Samuel Eliot Morison—helped create the American cruising tradition. These were yachtsmen-navigators who cared deeply for the sea, its ways, and its nautical traditions. Before reliable auxiliary engines, depth sounders, radio, radar, and loran, Tom Cabot sailed *Avelinda* downeast with his family for adventure along Maine's wild coastline, which provided adventure and honed his reputation as an intrepid and skilled boatman. *Avelinda*'s company was not drawn from professional mariners and paid crews, but, like his ancestor, John Cabot, from among those who were explorers by temperament and instinct.

Industrialist, statesman, yachtsman, family man, navigator, and adventurer are all pieces of Tom Cabot's remarkable life. But in the centuries ahead, Tom Cabot's most notable achievements will no doubt center on his philanthropic interests, which happily included an abiding interest in conservation on the Maine coast. Those who read the story of *Avelinda*, we hope, will be inspired by Tom's early understanding of how important the sight of a restless sea surging on a wild coastline is to the human spirit. Tom Cabot sailed his first vessel to Maine nearly seventy-five years ago, bought a score of islands, most of which he gave away, and helped convince thousands of others to follow his example.

Without Tom Cabot's vision, the Maine coast that we know today would look a lot different. Mostly outside of the public eye, Tom Cabot has established a legacy of what the Maine coast, its people, and its traditions can offer an increasingly small and congested world. And this unfinished legacy is an inspiration to all of us who follow in his wake.

Philip Conkling, Cynthia Bourgeault,
George Putz, and Peter Ralston

*P*reface

I hate to swallow ocean and it's all God's fault,
'Cause he might have put in sugar, but he went and put in salt.

I MUST HAVE HEARD THAT BIT OF DOGGEREL, OR SOMETHING LIKE IT, AS AN infant. My earliest memories, now somewhat obscured by the mist of time, are of a fear and a fascination toward the sea. My first ambition was to become a sailor like Sinbad, an Old Salt who would sail the Seven Seas and see the whole world. I wanted to explore unknown islands and tame the savage cannibals and wild beasts that I met, and to come home a hero to live happily ever after. The fairy stories read to me at bedtime were much more exciting than nursery rhymes. Killing dragons and three headed monsters was more fun than going up a hill with Jill to fetch a pail of water.

Now that I am ninety-five and have seen much of the world, I can dream about its oceans and spin a few yarns about seafaring. The ones recorded here are mostly true, but may have acquired a bit of embroidery in the frequent re-spinning.

At birth I must have had some salt water in my veins from my seafaring ancestors, but my father was a frugal Puritan who believed in hard work and not such a frivolous pastime as yachting. Insofar as I know, no ancestor of mine ever had a yacht. My father called yachts floating coffins and certainly didn't approve of my ever owning one or learning to sail.

By the time I got my first yacht, a gift from Grandma Moors on my thirteenth birthday in 1910, I thought of myself as an Old Salt. By 1919, when I made my first cruise down to Maine, I really was one. By then I had learned to navigate by the sun and stars, could use a sextant to determine the line of position, and could even calculate mean solar time from the lunar altitude. I was a veteran pilot at sea and in the air, had taught flying and aerial combat in World War I, and had navigated airplanes throughout south Texas and much of the Florida coast without any instruments, not even a compass. I had survived a dozen forced landings with a dead motor and lost twenty-seven of my colleague flying instructors.

At the war's end in 1918, I returned to Boston to finish college and to suggest marriage to my lady love, Virginia, whom I had met at dancing school before the war. She told me she wanted a family man, not a daredevil. It took me another year to persuade her that I could qualify as a family man, and now, after seventy-two years of wedlock, I'm still not sure that I've convinced her.

As a boy, my first taste of yachting came from the Anthony family who lived on the North Shore of Boston. Reed Anthony, my contemporary and ultimately my classmate at Harvard, would invite me for a sail on his father's big sloop *Doris*, which was moored off West Beach and had a hired captain and crew living aboard. These were only day sails and I was too young to learn anything much of seamanship. Also moored there off the beach was a knockabout owned by my father's cousin, Charles Cabot, whose son Elliot was a bit younger than I. They had a choreman named Chris who was Norwegian and had been a seaman on square-rigged ships from the age of twelve. Before I was twelve, we boys had been invited to cruise with Chris to many ports of Massachusetts Bay and I had learned a lot of seamanship, as well as navigation, sailmaking, and work with a marlinspike.

My three Moors uncles taught me about yacht racing. They were avid yachtsmen and founders of the Cohasset Yacht Club where they raced against such famous skippers as Charles Francis Adams, who raced cup defenders against British challengers for the America's cup. They jointly owned a racing sloop and occasionally asked me along as crew. It was they who persuaded my grandmother to give me a yacht.

My bent for exploration showed itself at the age of five when I ran away from home one sub-zero morning and was picked up in Boston and brought back by an uncle. Later I was sent to Camp Meriweather in Maine where I wanted to explore every nook in the shores of the Belgrade Lakes.

Now that I am too old to cruise, I have "swallowed the anchor" and live on an island off the coast of Maine in the summertime. It is Maine where I love to be and there where we spent forty summers cruising the coast on the big blue yawl *Avelinda*, designed by John Alden and built by the master shipwright, Harvey Gamage.

Thomas D. Cabot

AVELINDA. (Photo by Morris Rosenfeld, 1948)

CHAPTER 1

*W*atery Beginnings

I Was Born In The Reign Of Queen Victoria, Whose Navies Forged The British Empire and the Pax Britannica. Her navies kept the world at comparative peace for nearly one hundred years. I clearly remember her death in the summer of 1901 and the shooting of President McKinley that same summer when I was four years old. I also dimly remember some of the after-glory of victories at sea in the Spanish War which gave the United States the Philippines, Cuba, and Puerto Rico. In that year we had summered at Beverly Farms on the North Shore of Boston, but my first three summers were spent at Grandpa's big stone house in Cohasset on the high promontory of the bold south coast of Massachusetts Bay. We continued to visit there often. It was a delightful place with a covered porch running all the way around on which we could roller skate, bicycle, and even drive a cart pulled by an amiable goat.

My most important memory of this fabulous house was the brass telescope mounted on a tripod through which we could see the big ships coming and going from Boston. That was the age of sail. We sometimes saw as many as a hundred great ships under sail in a single day—even more when there was a northwest wind following days of easterly storm when ships could finally clear the harbor.

Grandpa and his three unmarried sons knew all the vessels, their cargos, where they were from, and where they were going. They even knew the captains and supercargos, for they were in the business of financing imports and exports. We learned all the different rigs: the full-rigged ships, the barks and barkentines, the brigs and brigantines, and the fore and aft rigged schooners, the newer ones with five or six masts, and the big *Thomas W. Lawson* with seven. The square riggers and larger schooners brought goods from the ends of the earth: hides and grains from the River Platte; tea from Shanghai or Calcutta; wool from Punta Arenas, Sydney, Christchurch; sugar and molasses from Havana; bananas from Cortes, Banes, or Port Antonio; rubber from Manaus; and coffee from Rio, Santos, or Cartegena. The smaller coastal schooners operated in cabotage, where foreign ships were banned, bringing lumber from Bangor, Machias, and Calais in Maine; or granite from Stonington on Deer Isle; or cotton from Savannah and Charleston.

To my uncles the news of ships arriving was the first thing to look for in the *Boston Herald* or the *Evening Transcript*. Is it any wonder that we came to feel some of the same excitement, even when we were too young to think of running off to sea? We had heard our parents tell of how ancestors had made fortunes in the China trade, or become ship captains by the age of 20, or

Age of Sail. (From a glass negative taken by the author about 1914)

sought adventure whaling in the southern seas, or sailed as privateers and taken rich prizes. Our family library was full of books on sea adventure, books like *Treasure Island, Robinson Crusoe, Twenty Thousand Leagues Beneath the Sea, Two Years Before the Mast, The Riddle of the Sands*, and *Moby Dick*. There was non-fiction as well and books of exploration by Slocum, Nansen, Amundsen, Peary, Shackleton, Steffanson, and Frobisher.

Grandpa Moors had come from a farming family that had settled in Groton, Massachusetts, early in the eighteenth century. They did pretty well growing wheat there for the Boston market until railroads from the Midwest brought cheaper wheat to Boston. His grandfather was one of sixteen children and there was little money left for him in the family when he came to Boston before the Civil War to serve as a clerk in a five-and-ten-cent store. There he saved his pennies to invest in a patented copper toe that was specified for Union Army boots in the Civil War. This gave him the money to build that showy house in Cohasset in 1867.

The Boston Cabots came to Massachusetts a bit later and settled in Salem in 1700. They did well in shipping, but my great-grandfather became really rich by marrying the daughter of Thomas Handasyd Perkins, who had made a fortune as a ship owner and trader. Before I came along, three generations of large families had so subdivided the fortune that we lived very simply in a four-family house in Cambridge. My father did well enough in business to put his children through Harvard where I studied engineering. It was at Harvard and MIT that I received the training for a profitable career as an industrialist. This earned me money enough to build *Avelinda* in 1936 and to spend forty summers cruising in her on the delightful coast of Maine.

In Cambridge, where I was born and lived in the winter until I was married, my two best friends were Delano Potter and Alec Bright. Delano, the son of the head librarian at Harvard, was brought up on seafaring tales, as was I. By the age of six or seven, we were both begging nickels from our parents for the streetcar ride to "T" Wharf in Boston where the fishing schooners docked. It was easy to get permission to board the ships and hear from the sailors about storms and how to weather them. Delano was so entranced by sea tales that he ran off to sea when only thirteen and served before the mast on a square rigger, later becoming skipper of vessels under sail, freighting lumber from the Maine coast to southern ports.

By the time we were ten, we had made boats of wooden boxes which we paddled into deep water. In those days, wines, soap, and other household commodities came packed in sturdy wooden boxes; the age of paper cartons had not yet arrived. We had these box boats first in Cambridge on the Charles River and later on the North Shore at Beverly Farms. It was not long thereafter that my older sister, Eleanor, and I put our pennies together and managed to buy a canoe, which we paddled up and down the Charles. That canoe led to a career in canoeing rivers which paralleled my interest in the sea and ultimately led to writing with John Phillips a guidebook, *Canoeable Rivers of New England.* This, in turn, led to my designing the Grumman canoe made of aluminum, which became very popular after World War II.

When I was eleven and we were spending the summer at Beverly Farms, my mother asked me to build her a hen house. This I did and developed some skill with handling carpenter's tools. The following summer she gave me the lumber to build a skiff. That was my first attempt at boatbuilding and was

Young Tom with three uncles helping to launch his first skiff built at age twelve.

Tom (lower foreground) and friends on a cruise to New London to watch a boat race. (1915)

Running with the spinnaker set. (1915)

not altogether a success. I had taken the design from a handyman book for boys and had scaled it down a bit from a fourteen-foot design. I didn't know enough about boat design then to realize that I should have scaled down the length more than the width. As a consequence, the skiff was too narrow and rather cranky. It did serve me as a way to get out on the water, and it nourished my craving for a platform of my very own on the lovable and spacious sea.

Close to the time of my thirteenth birthday, the spring of 1910, my youngest uncle persuaded my grandmother to give me a small yacht as a birthday present. It was the happiest day of my young life, even though my father thoroughly disapproved of my getting a yacht of my own at this age. This vessel was one of the one-design fleet of wooden knockabouts known as Manchester Seventeens, built by Morse Brothers at South Thomaston, Maine. Although only seventeen feet long at the waterline, it had a self-bailing cockpit and a cuddy with two wooden bunks. I named the vessel *Tulip* and put out a mooring for her off West Beach in Beverly Farms where we were spending that summer. In early July, during a northeast storm, the screw shackle connecting the mooring chain to the pennant let go, and, to my dismay, the vessel came in on the beach where the surf banged it to the point of breaking two ribs and some of the planking. My mother put up the money to salvage the vessel and have it repaired. It was a lesson I never forgot. In a lifetime of sailing I have, of course, had other vessels grounded, but this is the nearest I ever came to a complete shipwreck.

Soon *Tulip* became the boat to beat in the Manchester fleet. We also raced at Marblehead and Cohasset, and I still have in my cellar a collection of the mugs we won in those days.

Tom Cabot's Tulip *out sailing a four-masted schooner in the Fox Islands Thorofare.* (From a glass negative taken in 1919)

CHAPTER 2

*E*arly Voyages East

ONE DAY IN 1915 CAPTAIN JOSHUA SLOCUM, WHO WROTE *Sailing Alone Around the World*, which I had read as a youngster, anchored his boat in Salem Harbor. I happened to be out in my skiff when a squall came on and it started to rain. Slocum motioned me to come aboard, since he thought I might be in danger in the small skiff. He must have been in his seventies then, and was a great big fellow with a bushy gray beard. I was very impressed that he had sailed his heavy yawl around the world. I wanted to learn everything I could about boats. As we sat out the squall, he told me how he handled maneuvers such as heaving to in storms. He gave me a lot of tips about weathering storms at sea. One of the amusing stories he told was how he spread tacks on the deck when he was at anchor and worried that he might be boarded at night by unsavory characters; on several occasions this precaution had led to his awakening at night after a great racket on deck.

* * *

The worst wind I encountered in Massachusetts waters in my early years was at the start of my sophomore year in college, during a stay at Vineyard Haven on Martha's Vineyard. An older friend had chartered a large catboat with a one-cylinder engine, and about a dozen of us sailed it to Menemsha, six miles to the west of Vineyard Haven, for a picnic while a couple of the parents met us by touring car. By late afternoon heavy black clouds were approaching, and it was decided that the girls would return to Vineyard Haven with the parents by auto. The boys set forth in the catboat to Vineyard Sound with three reefs tied in the sail. When the storm hit us, it was far worse than we had expected and we had to lower the sail and tie it down. We started the engine, but it overheated and gave up. It was an open boat with no shelter, and the raindrops were so large and the wind so strong that we took a terrible beating. We huddled together under the furled sail. Spindrift and rain started to fill our vessel, and soon waves, too, were coming aboard. We bailed for dear life. We couldn't see and had no idea where we were. The engine having cooled, we managed to start it again, which enabled us to heave to so we were taking on less water. Our light clothing was soaking wet. We were cold and exhausted from bailing. After a few hours our engine quit again.

By midnight the wind had abated some, but we had no idea where we were and could see no lights. Shortly after midnight we were blown onto a beach. We pulled the vessel up out of the surf the best we could and planted the anchor to keep it from drifting off. Some of us were trying, without success, to light a fire with driftwood when we heard a cry that a light had been seen down the beach. We all ran to it and found a big house. We pounded on the door and a servant came to let us in. Soon the owner, Senator William Butler, came down in a dressing gown and immediately ordered hot buttered rum for all hands.

We were told we had been in a tornado and that we were on the beach at Lambert Cove, near West Chop. Many houses had lost their roofs and no telephones were operating. Soon a man was sent on a bicycle to Vineyard Haven to let the people know that we were safe. By dawn the roads were cleared with axes, and cars came to take us home.

* * *

When the United States entered the war in April 1917, my father, who founded the Massachusetts Naval Air Militia, was immediately commissioned in the Navy, and he sent my brother and me to a flying school near Buffalo, New York, founded by the Glenn Curtiss Company. My vessel *Tulip* was not commissioned in 1917 or 1918, but as summer approached in 1919, I found myself with a few weeks free before summer school started at Harvard (I was hurrying to complete my degree so that I could get married). With my college roommate, Alec Bright, I cruised eastward in *Tulip* from Beverly Farms as far as Frenchman's Bay in midcoast Maine. It was a memorable trip. I polished my skills at piloting and celestial navigation and learned a lot about the perils of anchoring and how to avoid dragging anchor if the wind freshened. We also had lots of experience finding our way in dense fog.

To prepare *Tulip* for the trip, we nailed a large wooden box to the cabin sole in which we stored our charts, provisions, cooking utensils, a small Primus stove, and our spare clothing. We had a kapok mattress which

Tom as an air cadet pilot. (1917)

19

Running east along the Maine coast on Tulip's *first voyage to Maine. (1919)*

roughly fitted the cockpit, a sailcloth awning to stretch over the furled sail at night that tied down to small cleats on the gunwale at either side, and another piece of sailcloth and a couple of blankets to sleep under. All of these were stored below decks during the day.

With a fresh breeze at our backs, we set off from Beverly Farms late one afternoon and rounded Thacher Island off Cape Ann before dark. We passed to seaward of the Isles of Shoals and Boone Island with its tall lighthouse. Shortly after midnight, the wind being aft, we were carrying the spinnaker and mainsail. While I was napping and Alec was at the tiller, he suddenly let out a yell and put the helm hard down. He thought he had seen breakers ahead. The spinnaker came aback and we had some difficulty getting it down. Wallowing in the sea with the mainsail flapping, we peered ahead, but could see no sign of breakers so we resumed our course toward the northeast.

Between 1:00 and 2:00 a.m. it began to rain. In pitch dark we put on our oilskins. The wind began to slacken, and by dawn it was flat calm. Our vessel was rocking severely in the remaining waves and we sat there, cold and mildly seasick, eating only a few bites of cold biscuit for breakfast. By noon the seas had subsided. We were miles offshore and there was still no wind. We decided to try to tow our boat toward the land with the dinghy. With one of us at the helm and the other rowing, we took turns at towing *Tulip* shoreward. We could see no recognizable landmarks on the shore and didn't know where we were. It was nearly dark before we were close enough to shore to identify some lobsterboats moored in what looked like protected water, and it was quite dark by the time we got among them and were able to anchor. We had only a small kerosene ship's lantern with Fresnel prisms, which

Alec Bright and Tom at the helm of Tulip *in the Gulf of Maine. (1919)*

Lumber schooner carrying kilnwood into Rockland Harbor for the town's lime kilns. (1919)

Years later, at anchor off Shackford Head, Eastport, with a raft of four-masted lumber schooners in the background in Schooner Cove where an oil refinery was proposed in the 1970s. (1938)

gave too little light for us to find anything much to eat or to bother with cooking. Having been awake for thirty-six hours, we had no trouble sleeping.

The next morning fishermen told us we were in Pott's Harbor (near South Harpswell), a little village with work-stained lobsterboats in the harbor. Although I had been to the Maine woods in 1906, this was my first view of the Maine coast from offshore. I found the combination of scenic beauty and utilitarian waterfront very moving.

It was a bright day with a good breeze and we sailed eastward around Cape Small, inside of Seguin Island, and came into Port Clyde in the late afternoon in plenty of time to cook some canned stew for dinner and have a walk ashore before dark. The next day we sailed on through the Muscle Ridge Channel to North Haven for the night. Pulpit Harbor, on the northern shore of North Haven, was already associated with another branch of the Cabot family. The first Cabot to summer in Pulpit Harbor was Walter C. Cabot. He had several sons, but the son who carried on the tradition was Henry Bromfield Cabot. Henry Bromfield Cabot had six children who were roughly my age. They've had I don't know how many children in total, but there are at least fifty of them who have houses in the Pulpit Harbor area. The original houses were on the southern peninsula, but they never built on the outer peninsula, which is now protected by scenic easements to preserve it from development. The inner peninsula has about six or seven houses on it, mostly of my generation. Then the innermost peninsula has about thirty houses, at a guess, where the next generation lives. These families have dominated that whole area of North Haven Island for many, many years.

Port Clyde's busy working waterfront with the old Wawenock Hotel in background. (1919)

* * *

We continued our cruise on *Tulip* through the Deer Isle Thorofare between Stonington and Isle au Haut to Burnt Coat Harbor on Swans Island. We went ashore for some fresh milk and bread at the small store on the shore near the wharf, which is now the fishermen's cooperative. The following two nights were spent in Northeast Harbor with a full day's sailing among the Porcupine Islands in Frenchman's Bay. We returned by way of Eggemoggin Reach, where we spent a night anchored off the north shore of Deer Isle, not far from where the large suspension bridge now serves that island.

I was struck by the beauty of the many small wooded islands, with the spruce trees growing at the margins of the rocky shores. We knew of the major harbors of the region and had found our way among the islands without mishap. These islands were a fresh, new world for me, an exciting revelation. Their wild loveliness strongly appealed to me. The fact that they were the first centers of fishing and trade hundreds of years ago, as well as early farming settlements, greatly interested me, too.

There was thick fog the following day as we left Eggemoggin Reach. We missed a buoy and got lost. We found ourselves among ledges and hit one lightly with no damage. We tacked into a light southwesterly wind all day in the fog, not knowing where we were, but occasionally seeing an island shore. Finally we anchored in the lee of a wooded island for what proved to be a rather restless night. It began to rain shortly after dark and by midnight the wind was freshening into a storm. We had only about fifteen fathoms of half-inch hemp rope tied to our anchor, which was the old fisherman's type. None of the modern patented anchors had yet been invented. The depth of water was much greater than we had anticipated, and although we were close to the shore, there was very little more than enough anchor rope to reach bottom. About midnight we realized that our anchor had dragged and we were adrift in deep water.

The longest line we had aboard was the peak halyard so we unrove it, attached it to the anchor rope, and got the vessel head to wind again, but we couldn't be sure in the dark whether or not we were still dragging. By dawn it was still raining although the fog had cleared. After some study of the chart, we found our position to be between Great Spruce Head Island on the west and the Barred Islands on the east. There was a large house on the northeast corner of Great Spruce Head Island, and we decided to row to it.

All our clothes were soaking wet and we were miserable and cold. We wrung what water we could out of our wet underwear, put on oilskins with nothing but underwear beneath, and in short order made it to shore. It was about quarter of seven in the morning, and a young boy and a girl our age were playing ping-pong on the screened porch. They asked us in, lit a fire in the living room, and invited us to stay for breakfast.

In this way we met the Porter family from Chicago, who had bought the Great Spruce Head Island in 1912. It was Nancy, the oldest, who had been playing ping-pong with her brother Eliot. Two younger brothers, Fairfield and John, soon appeared with their parents. We were much embarrassed, having only underwear under our oilskins, so before breakfast we got some more wet clothes from the vessel, and rowed back for a meal. We wound up staying all day and spent the next night in the shelter of their harbor.

I got to know the Porters later, especially Eliot the photographer; I still

The boom tent made of sail cloth over the cockpit of TULIP *kept us mostly dry at night.*

treasure several photographs he gave me over forty years ago of Great Spruce Head and the Penobscot Bay region. He was among the first photographers to use color, and I rarely saw him without a camera. Eliot's younger brother Fairfield became a well-known artist. A number of his fine paintings depicting the island and its inhabitants hang in the best museums around the world.

I also got to know Buckminster Fuller whose family owns Bear Island adjacent to Great Spruce Head. He was a class ahead of me at Harvard. Since I was trained as an engineer and he was trained as an architect, we could talk somewhat the same language. I liked him and I think he liked me. We used to talk statics. I knew the mathematics of structures pretty well and he, of course, made a specialty of this kind of thing. I was interested in his design of an automobile that steered by the rear wheel. It was teardrop shaped and built very lightly. He thought it was the automobile of the future, and I think it had some real influence on the design of automobiles thereafter, but steering by the rear wheel makes it very difficult to maneuver. He had some very good ideas and his designs of living structures are still well known today.

Maine islands have long attracted gifted people from away. They have been sought as refuges from the busy urban world, as sources of spiritual inspiration and nourishment, and as places of physical and adventurous challenges. My first cruise to the Maine coast was a voyage of discovery and opened a region of America to me that has profoundly influenced my life. I can't possibly remember the scores of cruises I had later and all the places I anchored, but I can clearly remember some of my misadventures and many of my favorite harbors and gunkholes. During that first cruise, though, the seeds were sown for my future involvement with these treasured places.

Son Louis taking sightings of the sun. (From a glass negative, taken about 1933)

CHAPTER 3

*F*amily Cruising

IN THE FALL OF 1919 I SOLD *TULIP* BECAUSE I WAS MOVING TO WEST
Virginia to start my apprenticeship in the gas business. The following May
I married Virginia Wellington of Weston, Massachusetts.

It was five years before I had a chance to sail again with regularity. In the
meantime, I occasionally crewed for others or acted as navigator in offshore
races. During those years, three sons were born and started growing up as sailors. Louis was born in 1921, Tom, Jr., in 1922, and Rob in 1924. Our only
daughter, Linda, was born in 1928 and Ned arrived fifteen years later in
1943.

In the spring of 1931, hoping to improve the helmsmanship, seamanship, and racing abilities of my sons, I purchased three eight-foot sailing skiffs
known as "rookies." These had originally been designed by the architect
Harry Shepley for his own children. We were able to get three of them built

Thomas D. Cabot and Virginia Wellington Cabot. (1936)

at a price of $35 each including the sails and oars. A fleet of these rookies became established at Cohasset and also at Marion, and for several years there was an intense annual competition between the two harbors in which the Cohasset team with three Cabots and one other lad managed to beat a four-boat team from Marion for several consecutive summers. Meanwhile, as our sons matured, we began racing against adults in the very competitive knockabouts of the Cohasset Yacht Club.

These rookies were light enough to carry on the roof of an automobile, and each year when school started we would bring them to our winter home in Weston for sailing and racing on a nearby pond. Once while sailing in a rookie with niece Lissa on Lake Cochituate, we met another tornado. We got our sail down in plenty of time to row ashore, but had to lie flat in the open amid rain to avoid the danger of lightning and falling branches.

I have seen a lot of different coasts in my time and sailed in a lot of different boats. The Maine coast offers a wide variety of beautiful and wild shoreland for cruising. West of Portland are long sand beaches dotted with cottages and crowded in summer. East of Portland, way east, long stretches of the shore are still primeval and appear from the sea as they did to the early European explorers. Rocky and indented with long bays, tidal rivers, and many islands, most of these waters are deep enough for cruising but not too deep for anchoring. Gerald Warner Brace wrote in his book *Between Wind and Water*: "There may be other coasts… The Aegean has been called the true realm of gold, but to a sailor of small boats it seems forbidding with its barren heights and depths. In Maine we have what are affectionately called eel ruts and gunkholes, and those with all the rest, even including the fog, make it the cruiser's true home."

In the late 1920s, I also had several sails in Maine with Dr. Alex Forbes in his large schooner *Black Duck*, whose homeport was Hadley's Harbor on Naushon Island in Buzzard's Bay. I was mate of the port watch, with Samuel Eliot Morison as mate of the starboard watch. He later became a professor of history at Harvard and a rear admiral in the Navy. On that first trip we sailed from Portland to Hadley's Harbor, and on a later voyage I sailed with him around Jeffrey's Ledge and back to Gloucester.

It must have been about 1928 when Alex Forbes asked us to visit him in Maine on Harbor Island at the mouth of Burnt Coat Harbor on Swans Island. A number of friends had visited him there during the war and post-war years, and he had organized these friends as the Harbor Island Club. On this visit he asked me to become treasurer of the club, a position in which I served for several years. Alex was a prominent physiologist and an accomplished skier and pilot. He bought Harbor Island in 1910, and during World War I let his friends use it. To allow them to feel freer to use the island, he formed the Harbor Island Club. It was a club in name only; Alex paid all the bills, collecting a nominal fee from members giving them the right to use the island.

To reach Harbor Island we took the Eastern Steamship Company's night boat from Boston to Rockland where we met another steamboat, the *John T. Morse*. Eastern Steamship's night boat left Boston around 5 in the afternoon and got to Rockland at 4:30 the next morning. In Rockland, you could connect with smaller vessels like the *John T. Morse*, which took you

The author recounts the following story shown in these photographs: "On a voyage in 1935 with several friends aboard the chartered yacht Phoenix, we entered Port Clyde harbor from the west. One of my shipmates believed he knew how to navigate the back channel into the main harbor used by fishermen. We struck an unmarked ledge inside of Raspberry Island on a falling tide. We tied Phoenix off as best we could. Waldo Holcombe and Sam Binnian dug clams while we waited out the tide.

But Phoenix rose again (facing page) under full sail off Eagle Island light in northern Penobscot Bay." (Note treeless Butter Island in background).

wherever you wanted to go in the midcoast region. The *John T. Morse* traveled between Rockland and Northeast Harbor, but about once a week it would make a stop on Swans Island.

The trips were fun. We had a good meal on the boat in the evening and got up the next morning at dawn to meet the *Morse*. Sometimes it was foggy and the captain would blow the horn as we approached an island trying to get an echo to determine our exact location. In very dense fog the boat would have to slow down, so that a fellow could heave the sounding lead to test the depth to bottom. Of course, there was a lot more risk in navigation than there is today. Now we have radar, Loran, and other devices to know our exact position. Then we made guesses in the fog based on the changing bearing of stationary sound devices such as foghorns, bells and, whistle buoys, but mostly we depended on a sharp lookout to see the shore before we hit it. Visits to Harbor Island gave our children a real love of that coast as well as some of their first experiences sailing in the fog and in vessels larger than a rookie.

One of the most exciting trips to Maine I ever made was in 1927 in the Eastern Yacht Club race from Marblehead to Rockland when I was asked by friends to act as navigator on a Q class yacht. We started off Marblehead Rock and were racing to the buoy off the Rockland Breakwater. Almost as soon as we left, we were in thick fog which remained dense until we reached Rockland. The most exciting moment was in the Two Bush Channel at the entrance to Penobscot Bay. It was about 10 p.m.; call it four bells. It was a very black night with very thick fog. The Bangor steamboat came barging through the sailing fleet and everybody started yelling and blowing fog horns and shining electric flashlights on the sails, hoping we wouldn't be run down by the steamer which didn't seem to have slowed down at all. Why the steamer didn't run one of us down, I'll never know.

Perhaps three hours later, when I was taking a nap, I was aroused by discussion on deck about a loud bell which was ringing somewhere in West Penobscot Bay (it would have been illegal for a vessel to blow a horn if at anchor). We finally decided it must be an anchored steamer of some sort. Later in the day, we discovered it was a destroyer which had been doing its time trials. I stayed on deck until we crossed the finish line and anchored in Rockland Harbor. We hadn't seen a buoy the entire distance across the Gulf of Maine from Marblehead until we got into the harbor at Rockland.

Beginning in 1932 we began chartering yachts for family cruising, not all of which were a great success. One charter in particular the whole family remembers. The vessel developed a smell of gasoline which we finally discovered was due to a leaky fuel line, but we didn't let enough vapor accumulate to endanger the vessel. I worried so much about the hazard and spent so much time on deck during the night rigging wind cloths to augment the ventilation below deck that I took sick before the end of the cruise and had to leave the navigation to our sons.

Our first family cruise in a larger vessel along the Maine coast was the summer of 1933 when we chartered a small schooner, *Porque No*, out of Camden. On the first day we sailed over to Great Spruce Head Island and anchored in the private harbor of the Porter family. Before dark, John Porter came alongside and told us that there was a radio prediction of high winds before midnight and that he thought we would be less exposed if we an-

With Virginia on an early charter. (1933)

37

Leaving Deer Isle Thorofare with Louis as pilot. Mark Island Light Station is in the background. (1934)

Entering Flint Island Narrows in Outer Pleasant Bay near Cape Split with Louis and Tom, Jr. (Tommie) studying the charts. (1933)

Virginia and Tom chartering with Louis, Tommie, and Robbie. (1934)

chored in Barred Island Harbor nearby. He offered to pilot us there. It was low tide and twilight. On entering the harbor we hit a sunken ledge halfway between the northernmost island of that archipelago (then called Peak Island by the fishermen, but now called by the family Escargot) and Western Barred Island. We were soon off the ledge and anchored in the harbor for the night.

It was our first night on the vessel and there were only four berths below deck. There being five of us, my son, Tom, Jr. was nominated to sleep on deck. He had a mummy-shaped sleeping bag with no zipper. He was only eight and not a strong swimmer. About 2:00 a.m. I was awakened by a call. I thought he had called in his sleep, but a moment later I heard splashing. I rushed up on deck. The rising tide was streaming by the vessel, and in the wake I could see astern something on the water. I dove for it; when I came up, I had only an empty sleeping bag. In a panic I started yelling hysterically. While the rest of the family swarmed on deck, I splashed around trying to find my son. After what seemed like hours, someone heard a faint cry from the bow of the vessel and there was Tom, Jr. hanging onto the bobstay, the only part of the vessel that he could get a hold of from the water. He and I were both pulled on deck with his wet sleeping bag, and he was put in my warm bed below deck while I was relegated to sit (with dry clothes) on the deck for the rest of the night.

The afterthoughts of that near drowning haunted me. From terror or cold, I'm not sure which, I shivered through the remainder of the night. In the beautiful dawn, I was near weeping with emotion. It seemed the most beautiful dawn I had ever witnessed and I resolved then and there to try to buy the surrounding islets. It was ten years later before I had a chance to do this.

On Norumbega Mountain in Acadia National Park looking out over Hadlock's Pond toward Northeast Harbor and Cranberry Isles. Louis, Tommie, Virginia, and Robbie. (1933)

Tom Cabot's Avelinda *at anchor off Yarmouth, Nova Scotia, at the stern of the steamship* Acadia. (From a glass negative taken in 1937)

CHAPTER 4

*A*velinda

IN THE SUMMER OF 1935, AFTER A FIVE-WEEK CRUISE IN A CHARTERED
ketch from Cohasset to the St. John River in New Brunswick and back, we
decided we ought to have a cruising vessel of our own. We now had four children and several nephews and friends who wanted to cruise with us, so we
thought we needed a vessel which would accommodate ten people without
too much crowding. We looked at several vessels to buy secondhand but
could find none we really liked. Finally we decided to build one new. I had
very firm views as to just what we wanted and made them plain to John
Alden, the famous yacht designer. He assigned responsibility to a young MIT
graduate in his office. *Avelinda's* six-ton lead keel was poured at the Harvey
Gamage Yard at South Bristol, Maine, in early December 1936. We sent
along a large British penny to be tossed into the mold for good luck.

    In those days Maine had the best shipwrights and the best woods in the world for building ships. Throughout the eighteenth and nineteenth centuries almost every harbor and tidal river in Maine had a shipyard that built merchantmen and warships, fishing vessels, and whalers for operation throughout the Seven Seas. On the shores of the Damariscotta River flowing past South Bristol you could find white pine, tall and straight for masts, white oak for frames, pine or spruce for spars, tamarack for knees, and oak or pine for planking. Men skilled with the adze, the saw, the plane, and the chisel would cut the tough wood, fit the heavy parts together, and hold them in place with trenails and bronze fastenings.

It was these skills and woods, in fact, that made the United States a world power—combined, of course, with the seafaring tradition of the Maine people themselves. One of the best tributes to the people of the Maine coast is described by Alan Shepard, the head of the Navy Memorial: "On June 12, 1775, in one of the first recorded naval actions of the United States, a party of Maine woodsmen, armed with pitchforks and axes, inspired by the news of the recent victory at Lexington, used an unarmed lumber schooner to surprise and capture a fully armed British warship off the coast of Machias, Maine. Captured guns and ammunition from the ship were used to bring in additional British ships as prizes. American raiders soon played havoc with British shipping all along the Atlantic coast. These actions—executed by ordinary citizens without commissions, letter of marque, or legal authority of any sort—began the proud history of the United States Navy, which was officially born by order of the Continental Congress on October 13, 1775." It was at Machias that Americans first began to harry the British shipping so badly that King George finally decided to give up his American colonies.

AVELINDA under full sail in Carvers Harbor, Vinalhaven, in the late 1930s while fishermen bait tub trawls for the long line fishery. (Photo by Montgomery Ritchie)

* * *

Harvey Gamage, then in his early forties, was the master craftsman who guided the construction of our dream vessel. Six feet tall with broad shoulders and large hands and forearms, he gave the impression of enormous strength and competence. He moved with agility, and though a born leader, he was taciturn, soft-spoken, shy, and never arrogant. He had a twinkle in his eye but rarely joked or laughed. His father was a carpenter who had built half the houses in the village of South Bristol, where they made their home. They lived near the mouth of the Damariscotta River, between Boothbay and Pemaquid, where a drawbridge serving Christmas Cove spans the narrow gut leading to John's Bay. Harvey fished and messed around with boats as a boy. A poor student, by the age of fourteen he had dropped out of school to help his father with his carpentry work. He took to building boats, while his brother Charles took to mechanical things.

They made a great team when fishing boats switched from sail to power. Their shipways on the shingle beach led into the cove from their great sheds with huge doors. In these sheds they built marvelous, durable wooden boats, taking orders for every kind, from small open boats for lobstering to large one-hundred-ton draggers for fishing on the offshore banks. In the 1960s Look Magazine published an article about Harvey Gamage and his work ethic. It commented about Gamage, "Work more than anything else shapes a man. If it is good work, it shows in how he moves within his family and within his community."

After World War I Gamage began to build yachts, but the stockmarket crash of 1929 ended that business. By 1936 Harvey was desperate for work and bid only $8,500, not including sails and auxiliary engine, for our fifty-foot yacht, although its specifications were of the highest calibre. Toward the end of the Great Depression, craftsmen who had the skills to bend the wood and hew it to an exact line with adze or broadax were paid only about one one-hundredth of the rate charged today. Boatyards such as Hinckley's at Manset, Wayfarer at Camden, or Robinhood on the Sasanoa can hardly find laborers with the old skills. Now that yachts are made of plastics, the old skills are rarely needed.

In World War II, the U.S. Navy badly needed wooden mine sweepers of a hundred tons or more, and the Gamage shipyard was awarded a multimillion-dollar contract to build a minimum of six. The Gamage sheds and ways were enlarged and priorities were granted for all the materials and equipment. Naval engineers provided designs, specifications, and the inspectors to see that the construction was properly done. The inspectors were strictly Navy and not from Maine. Before the first vessel was finished, tempers boiled. It is said that an Annapolis four-striper asked Harvey the size of the bronze screws being used for the planking and was told, "The right size." The Navy canceled the contract. But Harvey finished the vessel and four or five more like it, and each was accepted and paid for by the Navy when completed.

Before he died in the 1960s, Harvey told me that when he got the contract to build *Avelinda* he was so elated that he called his wife long-distance for the first time in his life. He also said the contract saved his yard and ultimately made him a rich man. Harvey left five daughters and a son, and for a long while after he died, his shipyard lay idle. However, a great wooden schooner bearing his name still plies the coast with shiploads of tourists.

AVELINDA *is launched at the Gamage Yard, South Bristol. (May 21, 1937)*

AVELINDA'S BIRTHPLACE: THE HARVEY GAMAGE SHIPYARD

AVELINDA was built by one of the most distinguished yards in the Northeast: the Harvey Gamage Shipyard in South Bristol, Maine. When in 1925 Harvey Gamage bought the yard—then known as the A & M Gamage Shipyard—from his grandfather, great-uncle, and uncle, the yard had already built scores of large vessels during the previous half century. There were no buildings in the old days—just several dozen very skilled men, and stacks of timber and sawstock by the water's edge. But Harvey Gamage had another idea, to build recreational craft for the growing sport of yachting.

When hull number one, a twenty-nine-foot Alden sloop named ACTEA, came off the ways in 1925, there began an extraordinary tradition of great boats built to the highest specifications. During the next five years the yard built forty-three yachts in lengths up to fifty-eight feet, with a boat list that reads like the lead articles of the yachting literature of those times. From the Alden boards came the schooners HALF MOON, MELODIE, SEA LADY, JOLLY ROGER, HAJADA, TYEHEE, WINDIGO, and ARCTURUS; and the ketches SCHOODIC, WEST WIND, and FOUR WINDS. ATALOA, WESTWIND, and WESTWARD came off Winslow's board, and STARLING and ALIBE from the offices of Burgess and Morgan.

Looking into the future, the yard began to build powerboats of its own design in 1930. By the onset of the deep Depression, power boats came to constitute half of the yard's production, all of these craft in generally smaller sizes than before the crash: in the thirty- to forty-foot range, with several craft less than thirty feet. Except for the yard-designed fifty-foot schooner FRANCES M, built

in 1932, AVELINDA was the largest vessel built by Gamage between 1930 and 1937, and no boat of such size would be built again until 1940, when the Eldridge & McInnis seventy-one-foot dragger DORIS ELDRIDGE was squeaked in just before the onset of World War II. AVELINDA was built during difficult times, but at the pre-war height of powers in the Alden office, and at the Gamage yard (the old-time wooden boatwrights were still in feisty middle age) when the very best materials were cheap and readily available, and the romance of old American yachting was still in an odd sort of bloom. Tom Cabot was a cherished client. He got a piece of the best before the world was swept into war and the nature of American yachting was changed forever.

* * *

The war had radical effects at the Gamage yard. It became once again a genuine shipyard, in 1942–43 building five ninety-seven-foot mine sweepers (both Alden and Eldridge & McInnis designs), two seventy-eight-foot P.T. boats for the Army (Eldridge & McInnis), and five boats for the Navy — three one hundred and three-footers and two seventy-eight-footers, all of these also Eldridge & McInnis designs. As did other Maine yards, it was during these emergency times that the yard built government-subsidized buildings to house and protect the work, giving the wrights and fitters indoor cover for the first time in three-quarters of century.

In 1944, toward war's end, the losses to the New England fishing fleet wrought by Navy and Coast Guard sequesters of working bottoms, plus the general shortages of foodstuffs in the country, created a national priority for working watercraft. Gamage went full time into the fishing boat business through 1947, building fourteen draggers up to ninety-four feet in length, and a host of smaller fishing craft. After 1948 and through the 1960s a few pleasure craft appear in the company roster, but most of the yard business continued to be devoted to working fishing vessels, most of them off Gamage's own design boards.

As wonderful exceptions to the yard's usual fare of draggers, scallopers, "fishermen," and lobsterboats, in 1964 appears hull number 228 — the beautiful one hundred eight-foot tops'l schooner SHENENDOAH; in 1968 the one hundred twenty-five-foot research vessel HERO (Number 238) for the National Science Foundation; and in 1969 the beloved sloop CLEARWATER (Number 241) for the Hudson River Sloop Society. During this era the yard began to work in welded steel as well as wooden shipbuilding, and the contracts for fishing boats became further leavened with contracts for other types of craft. The yard's last decade of ship construction began with the graceful ninety-five-foot schooner BILL OF RIGHTS. Amid the fishing boats appears the thirty-foot steel barge MOLOCH; the one hundred thirty-five-foot passenger vessel PROVINCETOWN; the HARVEY GAMAGE, a beautiful ninety-five-foot schooner; ZEKE, a thirty-five-foot tugboat; the thirty-two-foot Maine sloopboat LADY; and the one hundred forty-two-foot passenger ship AMERICAN EAGLE. The last boats built by the yard slipped off the ways in 1980, most notably the one hundred nineteen-foot high-tech dragger ARAHO built for F.J. O'Hara, then of Rockland. The final vessel on the company roster is hull number two hundred and seventy-six: WINDSONG, a fifty-four-foot dragger, launched in 1981.

The yard's spectacular record notwithstanding, it could no longer endure the boom and bust cycle that characterizes the marine construction business. Labor and materials costs had risen precipitously during the 1970s, abetted by a tripling of both marine engine prices and the cost of fuel to run them. Government subsidies for fishing vessels ended in 1980. Construction clients became more skittish and tenuous, and so the yard shifted its entire operation to yacht maintenance and repair. Today the big building sheds are dark museums of traditional shipbuilding. Great tilting-arbor bandsaws, planers, and jointers languish in odd corners, elder witnesses to another era when the din of a hundred employees reverberated around the harbor. The Gamages miss those times, especially the wooden boat revival days of the sixties and early seventies, when a new generation of young idealists appeared to take an interest in the ancient skills, and there were yet alive the old craftsmen to show them the ways of the work. For a magic decade old men put aside nostalgia, and returned to their tasks with a hint of immortality. But, then, that ended too.

The Gamage family is grateful for their modern customers— seasonal cottagers and their boats, some of which originally came off the nearby, now seldom-used, railways. Boats are hauled and launched via a twenty-five-ton travelift. In this era of black box electronics and rigorously monitored mechanical warranties, outside specialists are often brought into the yard for proprietary work. Business is manageable and steady, if not the same.

* * *

The design and workmanship of our vessel were both huge successes. *Avelinda* was built with white oak frames much heavier than Alden had recommended. The main timber was a single white oak piece more than twenty feet long and eighteen inches by twenty-four inches in cross-section. The planking was two-inch Philippine mahogany. She was fifty feet on deck, with five-foot draft, and a centerboard extended the draft to nine feet. The ballast was 12,500 pounds of lead within the keel. She was yawl-rigged, with the hollow mainmast and boom of Douglas fir and the mizzen of spruce. Her very tall mast with an unusual pitch to it gave her a silhouette recognizable from afar.

Most unusual as well was the huge propeller and large engine with a geared-down transmission. The twenty-eight-inch-diameter feathering propeller would push her ahead even against heavy seas. She could cruise at eight knots, and she had lots of tank capacity for extended voyages. She also had a very large and heavy rudder, and, with her long keel, she was easy to handle even in breaking seas and would hold her course remarkably well with the helm lashed.

In the fall and winter of 1936–37 we made frequent trips to Maine to oversee the building and rigging of our dream vessel. She was launched in the spring of 1937 and made her maiden voyage along the Maine coast in May. She would be our summer home for forty years.

We named the vessel *Avelinda* partly because we like the name Linda, which was the name of our daughter and my sister-in-law, and partly because my career in the Spanish-speaking American tropics had made me familiar

Cohasset to Monhegan in 14 hours! (August 4-5, 1938)

with that language. Friends familiar with Latin thought the name meant "Hail to Linda," but the name was intended to translate from Spanish to "beautiful bird."

We like to use the name *Avelinda*; we've had two other vessels by that name (we replaced our first *Avelinda* in 1975 with a 42-foot Whitby ketch built in Canada, and after four years that was replaced by a cat-ketch, built in Taiwan). None of our subsequent *Avelinda*s made of fiberglass and plastic were as seaworthy as the original made of good Maine wood and built by Maine craftsmen. We also have used *Avelinda* as the name of our forest lands in New Hampshire, Colorado, and Maine. Even in Weston, Massachusetts, we have *Avelinda* forest, marked with little aluminum signs.

When I was only a lad, I thought of cruising north as far as Labrador and maybe beyond into the ice floes. These dreams developed from my boyhood reading of the books by the Norwegian explorers Fridtjof Nansen and Roald Amundsen. Reading about the construction of their ships, the *Fram* and *Gioa*, had persuaded me to insist that the frames and planking for *Avelinda* be twice as strong as for a normal yacht. Alden predicted that the cost would be increased only slightly and the life of the boat lengthened considerably by this additional strength. It was a good choice. Unfortunately, however, the power, strength, and weight of the finished vessel led the Navy to use her for an icebreaker during World War II. The naval experts figured that her huge propeller and powerful Chrysler engine would push her up onto the ice and cause her thirty-five-ton hull to crush any ice likely to form in Casco Bay during the winter. She was requisitioned and sheathed with steel. She had two summers of offshore patrol for submarines and two winters

North by east; Linda at AVELINDA's *chart table. (1937)*

of ice patrol in the bay, but of course met none of Hitler's vessels. A glass doghouse over the cockpit and a coal-fired boiler in the forecastle kept the crew warm even in subzero winds. A radio was provided to report to base at South Portland any trace of U-boats and a fifty-calibre machine gun was mounted on the foredeck. A fisherman enlisted from Jonesport was appointed her captain. No doubt our dream ship would have given a good account of herself had any hostile vessel been sighted.

* * *

We mostly cruised in *Avelinda*, but when she was new, we successfully raced her. Although most of our cruising was in the Gulf of Maine, we took her as far north as Labrador and as far south as Chesapeake Bay. We had enough mishaps to provide many a good yarn for future gams. Adventure, by definition, is an undertaking involving risk. We took risks in our cruising because it is exciting; not foolish risks, but enough risks to have fun. We never failed to go to sea because of fog and rarely laid over a day because of a threatening storm. *Avelinda* was so seaworthy and so easy to handle that it led to overconfidence. Sometimes this got us involved in hazards of the weather and other misadventures.

I learned from sailing that the forces of nature have virtually no maximums. In tornados and hurricanes, the strength of the wind can become devastating. A 20-knot breeze, which is number 5 on the Beaufort Scale, can endanger small boats and calls for a warning red triangular flag on the mast of each Coast Guard station. I have been at sea when the winds reached 100 knots, causing forces more than 25 times as great. No man can stand unaided in such a wind. The forces on a jet plane at 500 knots are so great that if a man were able to put his head out of the window, his head would be wrenched from his body.

If you apply these forces to particles of sand which can be carried by a current of wind or water, the comparison is even more astounding. Only basic arithmetic is needed to make the calculation. The inertial force of any current, wind or water, varies as the square of the velocity. In addition to the inertial force there is some force due to viscosity or turbulence measured by the Reynold's Number, but this is negligible for ordinary comparisons. If the force per unit of area on the face of an object increases as the square of the velocity, the weight of the maximum object moved by the current increases as the cube of the square which is the sixth power of the velocity. With a tenfold increase in velocity, the increase in weight is a millionfold. If the velocity increases fourfold, the weight of the particle increases 4,096-fold; a 20-knot breeze will raise dust and fine sand while a 200-knot tornado will lift rocks a million times heavier. The importance of this is significant in understanding the enormous power of hurricanes, tornados, and rapid currents in the sea or river. When you hear of a tornado distributing the bricks of a house over several counties, you will better believe it.

In 1948 I sailed *Avelinda* with a crew of young friends from Cohasset to the Nova Scotia coast. We had planned to stop at Liverpool, but somewhere east of Cape Sable it began to rain and soon we were in a full storm. We decided to continue to Halifax. Of my crew all but Bill Binnian were seasick. We were uncertain of our position, but we could hear the signal of the Sambro Lightship on our radio direction finder. It was to leeward so we headed for it. We had furled all canvas as the winds were now hurricane force and our ship was almost out of control. We picked up the lightship and headed for the harbor channel making eight knots under bare poles. It was pitch dark and impossible to see the lights through the heavy rain, but somehow we managed to find the yacht club and anchored about three in the morning. All morning we lay there because we couldn't get ashore. There was too much wind to bring the vessel to the dock or to use our tender.

Years later in the new *Avelinda* we were caught at sea by the tail of another unpredicted hurricane on our way from Newfoundland to Nova Scotia. We left Port aux Basques at 5 a.m. after hearing radio predictions of sunny weather with light westerly winds. At about 10 a.m. when we were out of sight of land, the emergency channel of our VHF started broadcasting, "Security, security, security, calling all ships." This was followed by a series of numbers that didn't mean anything to us. I was sufficiently worried to call the Coast Guard on the emergency channel to ask the meaning of this warning, but was told I couldn't use that channel. Half an hour later, the same thing happened and I tried to take down the numbers, but they were read too fast. A large ship was approaching us which we identified as the ferry from Sydney to Newfoundland. I called its radio operator to find out the meaning of the warning. He hadn't heard it but had been spending the morning listening to rock and roll music. I asked if it meant there was some bad weather or if the Russians were coming and he responded, "Don't be ridiculous. Your vessel is a beautiful sight on such a beautiful sunny day." I knew that the Canadian government in its warnings to navigators used hertz numbers, but to convert hertz numbers into radio channels of a VHF set involves going to a reference book and I couldn't find such a book. Obviously it's not easy to look something up in a reference book when you're at sea in a small yacht. We later learned that it was blowing 85 knots in Halifax harbor that morning.

For us, the good weather continued until we entered the protected waters of the Gross Bras d'Or at dusk. When we got to Baddeck the next morning, the wind had escalated to nearly fifty knots and we were running under a triple reefed mainsail. Baddeck Harbor was filled with yachts and there was almost no room left. Luckily I was prepared with two anchors and sufficient cable ready. I rounded up, headed for the saltings to weather and dropped the two anchors just before we reached the mud bank. Snubbing to drop back, we fetched up within feet of the vessels tied to the dock. We were told that everyone on the dock expected a disaster and that the women screamed and men blanched.

In 1954, I had a wild experience in *Avelinda* with Hurricane Carol in Penobscot Bay. Because my usual family crew were all in Europe, I was alone with guests from the Middle West—a young friend, his wife, and two small sons—who had never seen a sailing vessel. They arrived at the dock with a steamer trunk. We struggled to get it into the dinghy, and then I asked my friend to get in so that he could help me load it onto the moored vessel. He stepped onto the dinghy's gunwale and "did the splits," falling between the dinghy and float. This half filled the dinghy and soaked the contents of the trunk.

The next day we were anchored in Crow Cove at Islesboro and in the morning it was raining, so we gathered some clams and set out for Castine to get other supplies needed for a chowder. I had been busy as cook and host and failed to turn on the radio to get a weather prediction. It was not blowing, but the visibility was low and I was occupied with the sails and piloting. After a while, there were some unheralded puffs which began to prove worrisome to the passengers, and I lowered the main. With shortened sail the vessel began to roll and the passengers all felt seasick. They retired below leaving me alone on deck, but this didn't seem troublesome as I was used to solo sailing. We were making slow progress under shortened sail so I started the engine. Soon the puffs became much harder and the wind veered to dead ahead. Fearing that the fury of the gale would shred the remaining sails, I lowered jib and mizzen. Even with my large propeller and using full power, the rapid increase in the wind and rising seas soon made the vessel somewhat unmanageable. My anemometer had already expired, and I later learned that we were near the eye of the hurricane and in the most dangerous quadrant where the winds were over one hundred knots. I did not dare reverse course for fear of being caught on a lee shore. The spindrift cut my face so that I had to keep my head below the coaming of the cockpit. By lashing the helm with about fifteen degrees of starboard rudder, I found that I could hold the vessel at about fifty degrees from the eye of the wind to starboard. With the centerboard down she seemed to be drifting approximately at right angles to the wind and parallel to the leeward shore which was only a mile away. Only occasionally could I get glimpses of this shore through the spume. Even under bare poles, the vessel was heeling, with the lee rail under water most of the time. There was little I could do except crouch on the floor of the cockpit with my face shielded from the sting of the spindrift, with the wheel lashed and my hand on the engine throttle, adjusting it with each gust in an attempt to keep the vessel from falling off the wind or broaching. I was powerless to tack, fighting to keep off the lee shore, and continually cursing my own stupidity in setting out without listening to a weather report, risking so many innocent souls who had had the faith to entrust themselves to my care.

I could only imagine the distress of my guests below deck and I was far from comfortable myself, lying in cold water, which sloshed inside my rain gear. After about six hours of this suffering, I realized we were coming into the lee of a wooded island; through the scud I saw to leeward the Sprague Oil docks of Searsport, which meant we were in the lee of Sears Island where I knew there was good holding ground in five fathoms of water. With the ship's knife in my teeth and my face close to the deck I squirmed forward to where my 125-pound Herreshoff anchor was lashed at the cathead, cut it away and let the heavy chain run out to its bitter end. I knew that this meant I had forty fathoms or six hundred pounds of galvanized iron chain to take the yank of the vessel when the chain came taut. With all that chain and heavy anchor, I was sure the vessel would come head to wind well clear of the Sprague docks.

Not long after I got back to the cockpit, the wind suddenly abated and the sun came out. I realized we must be in the eye of the storm and the next question was whether we would be clear of Sears Island when the wind backed to the westward. This it did and we were clear. I put out another anchor but we didn't need it. The vessel rode comfortably as the seas built up in the new direction. I was now able to get below deck to clear up the dreadful mess I found there and give what encouragement I could to the desperately sick and frightened guests. I doubt they ever went to sea again.

A fortnight later in Casco Bay we were threatened by Hurricane Edna, which followed a similar course and blew even harder than Carol. Again we were close to the eye of the storm and in the wrong quadrant, but we had an able crew and plenty of warning. We picked the shallow harbor of Jewell Island as the best hurricane hole we could find. We set a big Danforth anchor on a long and heavy nylon line to take a blow from the unprotected east, but it did little good because it fell (we discovered later) on a discarded oilskin jacket and never dug in. The center of this great cyclonic storm passed directly over us with winds officially recorded at 130 miles per hour. Twelve inches of rain fell, sinking nearby fishing boats with their open cockpits. Again the 125-pound Herreshoff held firm and with only seven fathoms of chain it kept our skeg from touching Jewell Island's southern shore, although the shriek of the wind and the vibrations of the whole ship left us near nervous exhaustion.

Maine gets few hurricanes, supposedly only one hurricane each century, although the twentieth century seems to belie that estimate. However, since this estimate is based on the long history of tree rings, it is not easily denied. The Maine coast has lots of lesser storms, but mostly in the winter, and rarely do the modern state-operated ferries fail to serve the inhabited islands because of bad weather. In earlier centuries when served by sail, islanders were often truly isolated in the winter and life on the islands was much less predictable and more hazardous than today. A visit to any old island cemetery will confirm this.

Shore party, Penobscot Bay.

* * *

My many years of cruising in *Avelinda* with family and friends were not all sailing offshore along the coast, or battling massive forces of nature. Visiting all the navigable rivers and little gunkholes into which we could float was a more varied pleasure and challenge, particularly those way down east, beyond Petit Manan Light. In these remote explorations of the eastern coast, we made friendships among the people we chanced to meet. The large blue yawl with its tall wooden mast got to be known and welcomed in every little harbor of that eastern coast.

Our ship came to be expected year after year in the long reaches and tributary lakes of the St. John River above the reversing falls; in the many rivers and harbors of Passamaquoddy and Cobscook Bays where we met great challenges; in Haycock Harbor above its perilously narrow entrance; in Cutler where we were most at home; at our own Cross Island, which we bought in 1941; (story to follow in the next chapter); in the anchorages of Machias Bay and its two great rivers; or in the Little Kennebec.

Of course we nearly always passed through Roque Island Harbor and often visited friends there, and traversed one of the two narrow western entrances to the lovely curved beach of fine white sand where we could swim or dig a mess of huge sea clams for a delicious chowder. Almost on her own *Avelinda* knew her way into the Cow's Yard, a protected anchorage off Head Harbor Island, and, if the tide was right, through the back channel to Jonesport where we also felt at home and usually bought supplies.

We had many favorite anchorages among the wild islands between Moose Peak and Petit Manan lights. Before the bridge was built, we used to

Roque Island beach.

Linda at the helm as a teenager. (1943)

sail through Moosabec Reach; our opposing its construction was of no avail, however, and the clearance was far too low for *Avelinda's* mast. We sighed when crossing westward over the Petit Manan Bar, for we were entering the region of summer residents. We felt that bar separated the men from the boys among those who sailed in yachts. We stopped in many lovely anchorages farther west, but it was never a perfect summer if we didn't get at least as far as the eastern end of Maine.

Of course we are not proud of the misadventures we and our vessels survived. We were sometimes a bit foolhardy and we had a lot to learn. In 1937, *Avelinda's* first summer, we cruised to the Magdalen Islands in the Gulf of St. Lawrence and on the way back met in Quoddy Bay a friendly yachtsman who had survived the war as a fighter pilot in the Lafayette Esquadrille. He had taken his yacht through the reversing falls of Cobscook Bay with the flood and dared us to do likewise. We were told to hug the point to port lest we be carried onto the ledge below. Too late I realized there was another ledge off the point with the churning white water falling over it at least six feet into the swirl beyond. No longer was it possible to pass to the right around it, but to the left was a V of heavy water flowing between the ledge and the point. With a yell for full left rudder and full throttle we passed through the V without touching and into the backwave which covered our deck and filled our cockpit.

Not far from the falls in Cobscook Bay, on the Little Kennebec, we had an even scarier mishap. We anchored in Moose Snare Cove at dead low tide. It was dusk and flat calm. We stopped when the depth of water was just five feet and dropped the anchor. We put out plenty of chain, but with no wind we must have been standing still and thus the chain landed on top of the anchor, fouling the upper fluke. After midnight we were awakened by a terrific jolt to our vessel that almost threw us out of our bunks. There was a roar of rushing water, and we scrambled on deck to find our mast among the leafy branches of a thick grove of trees and a white froth of water flowing rapidly past our hull. We quickly realized that we had picked up the anchor with the rising tide and drifted up the cove to the dam at the entrance of the millpond. We were headed upstream, into the flooding tide, with the anchor chain bar tight and the current so strong we couldn't loosen it even under full power. Finally, by rocking the vessel with the helm we managed to get the anchor loose and drifted backward into the millpond. In the morning it seemed incredible that we could have come backward through that narrow gate in the abandoned dam, and that our mast and spreaders had not snagged on the overhanging branches of the large trees in the old millyard. The anchor must have caught on the sill of the gate and when we recovered it we found the heavy shank had been bent a full ninety degrees to get free. After noon when the tide was high and slack, we passed back out into the cove.

An even more dramatic incident in the life of old *Avelinda* was when she got "hung by the tail" in Haycock Harbor. Haycock is our favorite gunkhole and there was hardly a year in our fifty years of cruising that we didn't spend a night there at least once. I think our fifty-foot yawl was the largest vessel that ever entered Haycock Harbor, and in all those years we never found another yacht inside. The outer harbor has needle-sharp ledges on either side of the channel that are invisible at high tide, and the passage

AVELINDA snug at low tide in the narrow gut of Haycock Harbor where she was once "hung by the tail." (1945)

through the shingle beach to shelter being only a tiny shallow stream at low tide, the approach must be made when the tide is nearly high. There is a wooden pile near the beach used by a local lobsterman to tie to while waiting for high tide, but it is hardly suitable for a vessel like *Avelinda*. Any vessel must maintain steerageway in the narrow passage through the beach, and if the tide is flooding this means a scary forward speed. Once inside there are cliffs to starboard and shoals to port with just room enough for a fifty-foot vessel to swing at anchor. There is plenty of depth near the cliff—about nine feet at low tide.

One summer day thirty-odd years ago, *Avelinda* entered the inner harbor at noon, about an hour before high tide, turned around to face the entrance, and anchored near the cliff. The youngsters aboard had challenged the adults to a game of scouting on our favorite point east of the entrance. While the game was in progress there was suddenly a cry from a sharp-eyed youngster that *Avelinda*'s mast was awry. We rushed for the dinghy but arrived aboard too late. The vessel had swung around at high tide when the current reversed from flood to ebb and her skeg had caught in a cleft of the cliff. We couldn't get it out. The stern was already several inches above the waterline and the tide had about eighteen feet more to fall.

We became alarmed that the outgoing current against the bow would twist off the skeg and destroy the rudder, so we set bow anchors to hold the bow firm and prevent it from turning in either direction. Then, as the bow sank and the skeg came above the water, we worried that the vessel might roll over sideways. There were very tall spruce trees above the cliff, so hoisting lines to the masthead and climbing high into several of the tallest trees, we pulled the lines taut so the vessel couldn't roll in either direction. Unfortunately, we didn't mark at the base to which trees we had tied the lines.

By six that evening everything loose in the vessel, including the bilgewater, had fallen into the forecastle and filled the chain locker. Our oldest passenger was propped in her bunk head up at forty-five degrees and unable to move. We couldn't get a proper supper and had been too busy to take lunch. At nine at night it started to rain and by ten it was pouring. The keel was in the rising water and there was no longer a danger of rolling over. But how could we untie those lines made fast high in trees? It was pitch black and we didn't know which trees to climb. All hands spent the next two hours climbing like monkeys among the branches and groping for knots in the heavy rain. By midnight the vessel was level enough to start the stove and serve hot drinks. By one a.m., as the tide turned, the skeg came free. It took until noon the next day to clean up the vessel and leave harbor on the next high tide.

* * *

We had adventures of other sorts. One hot, damp day, my wife and I were alone on board *Avelinda*, anchored off the northeast beach of Butter Island (near Great Spruce Head), which by then we owned. After breakfast we rowed ashore, pulled the dinghy up on the beach, and set to work building a trail on the island. We worked hard for about three or four hours, wearing only the briefest clothing because of the heat. We noticed that it was getting increasingly foggy and rainy. When we got back to the beach, *Avelinda* was gone. In the dense fog we couldn't see far, and we were rapidly getting very cold because we'd been sweating all morning.

We had no water or food with us. The wind was up and we didn't dare go far in the dinghy. We yelled for a while but that did us no good. After a couple of hours, then well past our usual lunchtime, a small knockabout with an outboard engine came up to the beach. We yelled at them and rowed out in the dinghy. What had obviously happened was that *Avelinda* had picked up the anchor with the rising tide and had been carried away. They loaned us some clothing because we were shivering badly, and took us downwind to look for our vessel. We stopped at various islands en route—first Bradbury, then Pickering—and went on down to Buck Harbor in Eggemoggin Reach, some four miles away. We couldn't find *Avelinda* anywhere. We hoped that her anchor would have caught on something and we would locate her somewhere along the shore.

We arrived at Buck Harbor at about 3:30 or 4 p.m. and were still terribly cold. People at the yacht club got us clothing and we found a friend who had a big boat with a VHF on it, who took me out looking for the vessel. Skirting the coast as far as Cape Rosier, we saw no sign of *Avelinda*. We contacted the Coast Guard, who put out an alarm; they had no record of her. Coming back from Cape Rosier in the dense fog, we could hardly hear the VHF because quite a big sea was running by that time. Finally we heard the Coast Guard broadcasting that the vessel had been discovered on the beach of "Hard" Island. I asked for its location, since I had never heard of Hard Island. At first they didn't know, but then they found it on the chart and said it was near Northwest Harbor on Deer Isle. Then I knew they meant "Heart Island." So we steamed back south toward Heart Island, but without radar it wasn't an easy trip in the dense fog.

From left: Virginia with Ned at the helm, (1948); pirate antics of Ned with Grand Manan in background, (1954); Virginia reads tales of adventure to Ned while AVELINDA is at anchor. (1952)

We got to Heart Island and there was *Avelinda* anchored in the lee of the island. It was still blowing hard and very foggy. I went aboard and found the vessel a shambles. She was hanging to the light anchor. We had a spare anchor, a Danforth, but the main chain was jammed. I went ashore at Parker's Point and talked to Gerald Warner Brace and his son Gerald, Jr., who had rescued the boat. They had seen the vessel coming onto their beach, and though her anchor had caught on the rocks, the water was shallow enough so that they could get behind her and push her off. They did a wonderful job keeping her off the rocks—the rudder and the skeg were undamaged. Then they got the engine going and took her in behind the island and anchored her. We got to be good friends with the Braces after that. I read all of Gerald Warner Brace's books about Maine—he wrote wonderfully well about the coast and its people. He was my kind of person.

With darkness coming on, I went back aboard *Avelinda*, got both anchors up and the engine running. My wife, Virginia, had been left at the yacht club. I motored along through the night and dense fog to Buck Harbor, using the fathometer to tell my depths, the compass to tell directions and a wrist watch to tell distances run. I found her at a friend's house and we thanked all the kind people who had helped us in a time of need and enabled us to find and save our vessel.

Of course, mishaps while cruising in Maine happened not only to us, and we were often able to act as good Samaritans to others. On one occasion, Virginia and I were living in a rented house near her sister Linda Perkins in Southwest Harbor. Virginia was caring for our infant son, Ned, and couldn't be away overnight. The members of the Northeast Harbor Yacht Club were planning their annual cruise and invited *Avelinda* to join. Their plan was to race to Prettymarsh where the younger members who were racing in open knockabouts would camp on the shore, and the parents would sleep on board the larger yachts. I persuaded Virginia and her sister to adopt a plan that would let us join the cruise, namely that Virginia and I would race our vessel and Linda would motor to Prettymarsh in our car, have supper with us, and spend the night aboard while Virginia drove the car home and returned next morning for the race back; Linda would then return home in the car.

We won the race to Prettymarsh and Linda was there to greet us. After dinner it started to rain. Virginia had left us and Linda and I had retired, when there was a knocking on the topside of the vessel. I went on deck to find a young man and five teenage girls in a dinghy asking for help. They were all sopping wet and blue with cold. Somehow, they had upset the dinghy and been dumped into the icy Maine water with all their food, blankets, and spare clothing. We got them aboard, found them such dry clothing as there was on *Avelinda*, rolled them into dry blankets, and put them in bunks with mugs of hot buttered rum. We gave them breakfast in the morning. After they had said good-bye, it occurred to me that we hadn't explained that Linda was my sister-in-law and they probably thought "Mrs. Perkins" and I were "living in sin."

Alcohol is good for a chill only if one has come in from the cold. It opens the capillary blood vessels and warms the skin, but this dissipates the body warmth faster and can be disastrous if the exposure to cold continues. Under the conditions cited above, hot buttered rum was ideal.

Matinicus Harbor. (1945)

Tom Cabot, Photographer

Stored in boxes in the Cabot family home is an extraordinary cache of images spanning seven decades of world travel, leading from China to Colorado, from the Alps to Antarctica. But it is clear that the Maine coast is the spiritual base for this large, well-traveled family. The Cabot's Maine collection numbers more than two thousand photographs. And while many of them are the very personal snapshots that a family accumulates in the course of travel and adventure, there is an overall quality and depth, as well as an undisputed historical significance, that rises well above the caliber of all but a very few personal collections.

The color images reproduced here are historically significant for another reason as well: Among them are some of the earliest color images ever made of the coast of Maine. Ever the pioneer, Tom Cabot began to work with Kodachrome in the mid 1930s, in the very first years it became commercially available. This large slide collection is an archive in its own right and demonstrates the remarkable stability of the Kodachrome transparency medium. While some of these images are now more than fifty years old, their colors are vivid, bright, technically perfect.

The inherent beauty of these landscapes, and the intimate feeling of being aboard with this unique family as they cruised the Gulf of Maine all add to the legacy of this remarkable man.

Lobsterman and dory in Scallop Cove, Swans Island. (1944)

Cutler Harbor from Neal Corbett's wharf looking at Little River Island and Western Head, protected by a Maine Coast Heritage Trust acquisition twenty-seven years after this photograph was taken. (1962)

The author recounts: "While cruising the Nova Scotia coast west of Canso we sailed up a tidal river and came upon a drawbridge that hadn't been opened for two or three years. We managed to get it unnailed by hand, but we had to get a horse to open the bridge wide enough to let AVELINDA *through. Virginia and a friend, Ruth Holcombe, went ashore to ask these women to lend their horse to help with the bridge." (1948)*

Agricultural land in the Canadian Maritimes. (1949)

Photographs, left to right: Ned and Virginia in heavy weather, (1952); underway in the fog, (1949); at the helm of Avelinda. *(1949)*

Dark Harbor off Grand Manan, which can be entered at high tide through a narrow hole in the beach cut by fishermen to trap herring on moon tides. (1950)

Criehaven Harbor in outer Penobscot Bay. (1940)

Penobscot Bay fishermen cutting birch brush for a herring weir. (1949).

Baiting tub trawls, Lunt Harbor, Frenchboro. (1964)

Virginia and Linda with friends on a favorite beach on Yellowhead Island in Machias Bay. An eagle's nest was situated on the headland to the right and the main part of the island lay off to the left. The author thought about bringing AVELINDA *into this cove and tying her off to the cliffs, but his crew dissuaded him. (1941)*

Virginia and Ned on the shores of the Brothers Island in Machias Bay looking east to Libby Island Light. (1950)

Northeast beach of Butter Island. (1949)

The Barred Islands off Butter Island; looking northwest from Bartender to Escargot islands which the author's family named after acquiring them. (1966)

On Butter Island with Beach Island in background (on right). (1975)

* * *

Our cruises to Maine were always full of adventure, which was the reason we kept returning to the bold rugged coast year after year. I had tremendous confidence in the strength and seaworthiness of *Avelinda* which allowed us to go to sea with the knowledge that our vessel could withstand most of all the forces of nature that visit the Gulf of Maine. But my closest brush with the devil or the deep blue sea had nothing to do with hurricane winds or groundings in the fog.

On the last day of our earliest voyage returning from Maine, we entered Newburyport Harbor. In between the jetties and in a deep part of the harbor, we decided to anchor. I went forward to set the fisherman's anchor. Just as I threw it overboard, the fluke of the anchor caught in the pocket of my trousers and pulled me with it off the deck. I went down very quickly with the anchor in about twenty-five feet of water to a mud bottom and started struggling to get free. It took me perhaps fifteen seconds to get the fluke of the anchor out of my pocket. I was scared pink because I was down there in the mud with very little light. I got free and swam up to the top, but I had the scare of my life; and ever since, I cannot help but remember the episode whenever I am up on the foredeck preparing to anchor.

Wharf Point at Southeast tip of Butter Island during its Dirigo Island Resort heyday in the 1890s.

BUTTER ISLAND: ROCK, WOOD AND FIELDS

Today the natural history of Butter Island is almost inseparable from its long history of human use following European discovery of the rich resources of the coast and gulf of Maine in the late sixteenth and early seventeenth centuries. Settlement of some of Maine's islands began as early as 1614, in the case of Damariscove off Boothbay Harbor, or shortly thereafter for Monhegan and Matinicus. But for most of the Maine islands, like Maine itself, permanent settlement was delayed for another century and a half by the long, bitter, brutal warfare between the English on one side and the French and Indian allies on the other who vied for control of Maine's vast natural resource treasures.

Following the fall of Montreal in 1760 which ended the French and Indian Wars, the population of coastal Maine began to explode as settlers poured across America's first frontier into the newly secure eastern territory of Maine to farm and fish, to build boats, and to establish maritime trade routes that would carry Maine products along the Atlantic shores and later around the world.

Butter Island was first settled in 1778 during the Revolutionary War according to Charles McLane's meticulous history of this and other islands of midcoast Maine.* The significant natural feature of Butter that most probably explains its name is the presence of a large bog, several acres in size, which the island's early inhabitants "improved" by damming to create a sizable farm pond. This improvement meant that water for livestock— a relatively scarce commodity on islands of a few hundred acres— was abundant and could sustain a larger number of milking cows

for the production of butter and cheese than on other Penobscot Bay islands.

For most of the nineteenth century, Butter Island was dominated by the Witherspoon family who were among the most successful farmers to settle the islands of Maine. John Witherspoon and his son Unadilla, who succeeded him, cultivated over two hundred acres of Butter Island's two hundred and fifty acres, and maintained according to McLane some twenty-five cows, six oxen, and over two hundred sheep and pigs. Like the islanders on nearby Great Spruce Head, Bear, and Eagle islands, the Witherspoons no doubt supplemented the family larder and trade with lobsters and herring from inshore fishing operations. Although the Maine islands seem distant today, during the Age of Sail the maritime version of Route One was literally at islanders' doorstep and deep water channels connected Butter Islanders to the rest of the world.

Many other Maine islands in the nineteenth century were settled and improved by the prodigious industry and frugality of their residents, but the land and soils of Butter Island were unusually deep and fertile as a result of their unique geography. Two large headlands rise up along the northeast shore of Butter connected by a high saddle that runs between them. The land then slopes gently southwestward from these promontories, and it is easy to visualize how deep soils were deposited by the glacier at its downstream edge. Where these deposits came into contact with the sea, they were sorted and reworked by wave energy producing a series of fine sand and gravel beaches clockwise from Wreck

Picking flowers on Butter's high hillside looking west toward the Camden Hills in the late 1940s.

Beach (on the North) to Orchard Beach, Nubble Beach, South Beach, and finally to Shelter Beach on the west.

After supporting three generations of Witherspoons, Butter was sold to a pair of Bostonian architects, the Harriman brothers, who created a large summer resort on the island. Soon the farm landscape was transformed to offer golf, tennis, swimming, hiking, sailing, and picnicking activities for their upscale Boston guests who arrived on the overnight steamer that brought them (with a change in Rockland) to "Dirigo Island" (from the state motto "I lead") as the Harrimans fancifully renamed the island.

The Dirigo Island Resort era lasted for two decades from 1896 to 1916. In 1916 when the Eastern Steamship Company, which had aggressively expanded its routes throughout all of New England and into Long Island Sound and New York, began retrenching, ferry service to the Dirigo Colony was suspended. Without convenient transportation, the colony virtually folded up overnight, and buildings began to be disassembled and floated off to other islands. Although sheep remained for a time, they, too, began to disappear from a combination of old age and the nearly irresistible attraction of free mutton on a nearly deserted island.

By the end of the 1980s, only a few acres of cleared land remained around the top of the headland above Nubble Beach. The fields and pastures have been replaced by fast growing white spruce, and these trees have already begun to be harvested by maritime windstorms, which are as efficient a woodland force as any woodcutter. In the spruce forest, deer, not sheep, prevail. But throughout the wooded interior are stonewalls, cellarholes, overgrown cart paths, a stone-lined bubbling spring, a lilac-shrouded cemetery, and scores of other reminders of the energy and industry of the family that first turned the island's abundant natural resources to human ends.

Today, perhaps the least changed piece of Butter Island is the towering headland above the island's most beautiful beach. The top of this headland provides the most stunning panoramic views in all Penobscot Bay. Not only are scores of small island worlds revealed from this aerie, but the outlook encompasses the wide panorama of Maine's grandest seascape from Stonington and Isle au Haut to the shores of North Haven and Vinalhaven, and across the western horizon to Rockland Harbor sixteen miles away where each afternoon the sun falls off the edge of the known world.

It is over this headland that the spirit soars, where the swiftest wings of hawks and falcons cut the air, where all eyes are alert to all movement, and where generations of stewards of this family island have surveyed an incomparable Maine island realm. From this headland one sees both the hand of man and the hand of nature and knows that they are of one body.

* McLane, Charles. Islands of the Mid Maine Coast, Vol. I. *Woolwich, Maine: Kennebec River Press, 1982.*

Avelinda at anchor off the outer shore of Brimstone Island off Vinalhaven. (1945)

CHAPTER 5

*A*ngling for Islands

EVERY YOUNGSTER DREAMS ABOUT ISLANDS; I WAS NO EXCEPTION. MY dreams persisted, and I was fortunate enough to have many opportunities later to own islands, including the mini-archipelagos of Butter Island in Penobscot Bay and Cross Island in outer Machias Bay in eastern Maine. By the mid-1940s I had purchased forty-one islands off the coast of Maine. I got the reputation for being willing to pay $100 for any good-sized island with woods on it, and I had many offers. Although some of the islands were nothing more than skerries or ledges, seventeen had trees on them, and in all they covered about four square miles and more than a score of miles of shorefront. Their total cost was under $5,000.

It was fun collecting islands; I took great pleasure in owning them and pride in giving them away. I could have made millions if I had sold them for development. Since 1950 the market value of Maine islands has advanced by a factor of at least one thousand. I didn't make any such profit, but I didn't do badly considering the amount I saved in income taxes by giving nearly all of them to the federal and state governments. The best of my island holdings are held forever wild by the United States Fish and Wildlife Service of the Department of the Interior; all of the others are protected by scenic easements.

The first group of islands I bought were Cross Island and six nearby islets, including the Double Shots, Mink, Scotch, and Old Man off Cutler, the last islands in eastern Maine before Quoddy Head at the Canadian border. In the summer of 1941, as I lay at anchor in the northeast cove at Cross, a lobster fisherman, a squatter on the island, told me that a hunting guide from Machias was negotiating to buy the island from the Pejebscot Paper Company. By that time I had been up and down the coast many times and I knew most of the islands. I said to the fisherman, "If I had known these were for sale, I would have bought them myself." The following February, after the attack on Pearl Harbor, the fisherman wrote me—he was hardly literate—that I could buy the islands for $6,000, the guide having paid $2,700 for the lot of them. I replied I didn't want them at that price, but if the guide desired to get rid of them, I'd pay the $2,700 they had cost him. The fisherman then wrote that the guide had actually paid only $400, so I could buy them for $400, but I would have to pay off the guide's debt of $2,300. By now I had some money, had built *Avelinda*, and besides, the islands were cheap. So I said yes. A year later, after I had title and had explored all the island, I paid the fisherman a finder's fee of $100. Afterwards the fisherman and I became fine friends.

Cross Island is the easternmost large island on the Maine coast, at the junction of Grand Manan Channel and Machias Bay. It's a huge island: fif-

Tom on Cross Island's rugged outer shore with the Libby Islands in the background. (1945)

teen hundred acres at least, with big, high cliffs and a cave on its outer side, and many beaches scattered around its immense shoreline including a sand and gravel beach at Northwest Cove. An old Coast Guard station built in 1874 and abandoned in 1917 was included in the purchase and was in good shape at the time. When we bought Cross, forty Navy men were living in the modern station with a tower, which was built in 1917.

My son Tom, Jr., who was in the Navy designing radars at the Massachusetts Institute of Technology, had a three-day holiday in April of that first year of the war, and so we decided to visit the island. We took the night train from Boston to Machias, bringing with us a folding sea kayak decorated with a swastika, which I had bought in Germany before the war. As we set it up beside the Machias River, we had a difficult time convincing the gathering crowd we weren't spies. I had notified the Navy men on the island that we were coming but not the security people in Machias, who were ready to arrest us.

It started to snow as we paddled down the river and we encountered steep seas in Machias Bay with the outgoing tide. A picket boat from Cross Island came to greet us. We had trouble persuading the crew to let us go on rather than risk overturning us in an attempt to tow us or to take us aboard. We landed safely on the island and spent the night in a deserted shack. The next day we explored the shores of Cross by walking all around it—a full day's work. We were stopped innumerable times by raw recruits on Navy patrols, who, while keeping us covered with side arms, ordered us first to hold up our hands and then to place our credentials on a rock, which they examined before they allowed us to continue.

It took us more than twelve hours to walk around Cross, keeping to the shores. The interior in those days was so full of slash that you couldn't have walked through it. Today that slash is fairly well rotted. It's now fifty years since Cross Island was cut over. They took approximately 20,000 cords off the island between 1938 and 1940. Although I've never trained as a forester, I know that to cut pulpwood in a wild, exposed forest such as on Cross Island, you've got to do it as a clearcut. It is very difficult to cut selectively because the trees are growing on the steep hillsides with many big ledges and are subject to blowing down after the first big wind. The Maine islands, like the Maine woods, have been a great source of wood pulp. Hundreds and hundreds of the Maine islands have been bought or leased or cut by the paper and timber companies for the forest products industry over the past century and a half.

In the course of this long walk, we met the two Dobbins brothers, Will and Rob, who lived on opposite sides of the island. I was aware that they had been feuding for years over the rights where each could place his lobster traps in the waters surrounding the island. I told them they could continue to occupy their cabins only if they stopped feuding and agreed to act as caretakers for the island. They would pay one dollar a year rent for their respective cabins, thus voiding the question of squatters' rights. For some years thereafter the two brothers continued to live peacefully on the island. Will was never allowed ashore by any of the women who lived with him because he would get drunk. I gave him a bottle of sherry once for rowing me across his cove when I'd left my boat on the other side and didn't want to walk, which his woman friend did not like at all. Their reputations along the coast were far from exemplary, and there is little doubt that trouble with the law caused them to

Lobstering with Will Dobbins at Cross Island. (1945)

live in self-imposed exile as hermits. They had plenty of chances to take ad-
vantage of me, but I came to feel them trustworthy with respect to any liquid
assets, unless contained in a bottle.

In addition to the fishing camps the Dobbins brothers lived in, there
was another shack which I later bought. I paid $75 to a fellow who had built
it out on Grassy Point because he had some rights in connection with it, and
I wanted to clear up the title. All the windows had been knocked out, and it
was somewhat skewed because the wind and waves had hit it. Something
could have been made of it, but it's long since blown away.

On our walk, we saw the sea cave in the cliffs on the outer shore, which
you can enter only at low tide after scaling down some cliffs. It's a long, narrow cave that seems to capture the restless beat of the sea. With sunlight
pouring in and just the immense sea as a view, it's like being in a chapter of
Treasure Island. We also discovered the water-filled hole of an abandoned
copper mine. We noted cellar holes of the houses of former inhabitants. Several families had lived on the island in the nineteenth century and done well
by fishing, farming, mining copper, and selling supplies to the coasting
schooners that sought shelter in the coves. Sheep belonging to a retired sea
captain were pastured on the grassy shores, and we observed that some of the
interior woods were accessible by passable roads built for recent logging.

We spent the second night in the abandoned surfboat station on the
beach seaward from the more modern station occupied by the Navy. Still in
good repair, it had potentialities as a peacetime summer home. Unfortunately, it was completely vandalized before we could realize this. The station
was built when lumber from eastern Maine was carried to southern ports by

Cross Island's original life saving station built in 1874 in the eastern cove and abandoned in 1916 for the newer station located on Cross Island Narrows. (Reproduced by permission of the Mystic Seaport Museum, Inc.)

This once elegant life saving station continues to be reclaimed by the forces of nature. (1945)

fleets of schooners without power or modern aids to navigation to reduce the peril of shipwreck. Strong and valiant oarsmen were needed to man the surf-boats stationed on the outer coast during winter storms.

The newer station, with a marine railway and diesel-powered surfboats, was built in 1917 on a five-acre lot taken by condemnation. It was located on a more protected shore and continued operation under the Coast Guard for some years after World War II. We enjoyed the friendship of the Coast Guard personnel during this time. One evening two of these friends came aboard Avelinda for cocktails. It was cold and when they left to return to the Coast Guard picket boat, which was moored near us, they slept that night with the hatches closed. The next morning they were found in their berths dead from carbon monoxide poisoning. At the Coast Guard hearing in connection with this tragedy, I was asked to testify that they were not intoxicated when they left us. Others had already testified that they had gone to Cutler and played several games of pool after they left us, so this hardly seemed necessary. Since this experience, I have always been afraid of coal stoves in an enclosed cabin.

When the Coast Guard abandoned the station in the 1950s, I tried to buy the five-acre reservation and buildings. After some frustration, I surmised that there might be a flaw in the title. Eventually, I discovered that the government had lost a case in another state where a lot had been taken by eminent domain for a lighthouse and the former owner had successfully claimed reversion rights when the light was abandoned. It was obvious that on Cross Island the cost of salvaging anything from the abandoned buildings was prohibitive. However, I was able to get the government to accept a modest offer for the abandoned station and the land around it. In 1968, I gave the buildings and a somewhat larger lot to the Hurricane Island Outward Bound School. The school needed an alternative to their base on Hurricane Island in Penobscot Bay due to a difficulty in renewing their lease.

* * *

Will and Rob Dobbins taught me a lot about the perils of the sea and the early glories of that part of the coast. Their grandfather had mined copper on Double Shot Island and had fought in the Civil War. They urged me to land on Double Shot and Old Man islands, which lie offshore of Cross Island in exposed locations and have no easy landing points. The cliffs run right into the sea and you can't tie up to anything—you have to go straight up to the rocks. They can be visited only in very calm weather; I think I've landed on them only three times in all the years since we bought them.

Old Man and Outer Double Shot islands have large rookeries of seabirds. More gulls and cormorants nest on Old Man, which has about two acres, than anywhere else on the Maine coast. Originally called Old Man's Ass, it was well-named, since it stinks to high heaven and has a hole through the middle so that at high tide it becomes two islands.

To fortify the American position in discussions with Denmark over salmon fisheries, the United States government needed more information on the habits of the anadromous Atlantic salmon. Accordingly, a program was started in the 1950s to staple inch-long nylon tapes to the dorsal fin of fingerling salmon smolt that are released annually in the Machias River. Each tape bore a number and a one-dollar offer to anyone returning the tape with information as to where the fish was taken. The office was getting few tapes re-

Will Dobbins (left) and friends have just landed this steer on the shore of Cross Island. (1948)

Will Dobbins' camp and lobster wharf on Cross Island between Northeast Cove and Berry Cove. (1941)

Virginia and AVELINDA *at the Double Shot islands off Cross. (1945)*

turned until one day a Maine fisherman brought in a whole bucketful. After making sure that they would pay him one dollar each, he revealed that he had collected them on Old Man Island. Imagine how much guano he must have sifted to earn the reward.

Because so many of the salmon raised at federal hatcheries were being eaten by cormorants and other seabirds on their way to the ocean, the federal government has been destroying eggs in this great rookery—an expensive and hazardous job on such formidable cliffs. Now the State of Maine, in an attempt to save the eider ducks, has declared Old Man Island a Critical Area and asked me to stop anyone from landing there during the nesting season. I have received more than two hundred pages of correspondence about this federal versus state conflict, which must have cost the taxpayers many more times than what the whole island is worth.

Shortly after I purchased Cross Island, I was able to buy one and one-half miles of shorefront on Thornton Point immediately across the narrows from the island. The land was being lumbered for pulp wood at the time. I offered one dollar an acre for the denuded land and paid the logger a few dollars to leave a fringe of trees along the shore. I got title from the owner of record.

A few years later, the Navy wanted the property for a radio station. I said I would give it to them if they would agree not to cut the fringe of trees. We subsequently agreed on a price but the Navy would not accept a quit-claim deed, and I refused to give a general warranty because of possible flaws in the title. This forced the Navy to condemn the property with the price stipulated. Years after I had received my money, I was notified by the Federal District Court that I had received it illegally. Although the Navy was satisfied, the court had discovered that the stipulation I had signed had not been signed by a claimant to a small lot included in the property. The court threatened me with judgments and even incarceration, and it took nearly two years of correspondence and conferences to cut through the red tape and get the federal attorney to absolve me. Now this Naval radio station is the largest in the world, with twenty-five towers approximately as high as the Eiffel Tower, making it the most conspicuous landmark along the entire eastern coast of the United States.

* * *

Whenever we stayed on Cross Island, we made a point of going into Cutler Harbor, not just to get supplies, but because we admired the industry and independence of the people whose immaculate cottages line the shores of this protected fishing village. One very foggy morning in August 1950, I met Judge Bailey Aldrich and his wife, Betty, of Tenant's Harbor in the store at Cutler. They were in a great hurry to leave in their tiny Friendship sloop because they had just heard that the highest tide of the year was due at 12:20, and there would be five feet of water in the manmade entrance through the shingle beach which forms Dark Harbor in the high, red cliffs of Grand Manan Island, New Brunswick, approximately twelve miles across the Channel. In clear weather, these great cliffs are visible from Cutler. When a half hour later I was back aboard *Avelinda*, I happened to mention this to my crew. The immediate response was: "*Avelinda* only draws five feet; let's go, too! We can catch them!" With no argument, the capstan was manned, the anchor weighed, and we steamed out of Cutler at flank speed. Two hours

The author recounts the following story of this photograph: "We landed on the rugged shores of Jordan's Delight Island and found a sheep stranded on a very narrow ledge. I stayed aboard AVELINDA while Virginia and a friend, Livingston Hall, assistant dean of Harvard, lowered seven year-old Ned on a rope down to the ledge to rescue the sheep. But the sheep became frightened and jumped into the ocean. In light air under full main, I hove to, upwind of the struggling sheep because the dinghy was ashore and managed to lasso the creature and haul it aboard. A sheep full of water weighs more than you can imagine." (1950)

First raven at Kent Island (off Grand Manan) with Ernest Joy.

later we heard a one-cylinder motor ahead, but they didn't hear us, and when we appeared out of the fog only yards away headed for their stern, there were startled screams.

We arrived first at Dark Harbor and sneaked in the narrow eel-rut into the deep salt pond behind the beach, where we anchored in seven fathoms of water near the cliffs. The spring tides had attracted many dulse gatherers, who could earn more than a dollar a minute in that cold water picking this delicate edible seaweed from the rocks uncovered by the subnormally low tide during the full moon.

Some herring fishermen offered a sightseeing ride of the island for the seven of us, including the judge and his wife, who had made it safely to the anchorage not long after us. We might have enjoyed it more if our tourguides hadn't driven most of the way with the accelerator of the old Ford pushed to the floor while they spun yarns of how we might not be able to get out of their harbor until the exceptionally high tides of the following August. But the next day we did.

* * *

Yellowhead Island, in Machias Bay not far from Cross, is the most beautiful island on the Maine coast. With spectacular yellow volcanic cliffs rising one hundred feet from the sea, topped by trees that make them them seem even higher, it is the most spectacular headland in the whole Gulf of Maine. An osprey occupies a nest in one of those very high trees, having taken over an abandoned eagle's nest when their populations declined from pesticide poisoning. To get to the highest point on the island, you have to start climbing from a gap in the middle of the island created by two incredibly steep, spectacular beaches that face each other. It's a difficult hike up to where the nests are, and the main part of the island is also quite hard to walk over, although a trail exists around the crest. The headlands each have a small patch of trees on the top of them. Because the slopes are so steep, there is very little fresh water on the island, although the present inhabitants collect water on the west side in a brownish sort of spring which they can use to wash dishes, but not for drinking. Drinking water is brought out from the mainland.

I tried to buy Yellowhead from Mrs. Foss, the daughter of the captain who pastured his sheep on Cross, in about 1948, when I was looking to buy the most beautiful parts of the Maine coast. I dickered with her all one evening. She collected scissors and I had to look at every pair—she must have had at least a hundred. She wanted $200 for the island; I figured I could get it for less, and I think the highest offer I made was $75. She later called me long distance and said, "Ah ha, I sold the island for $200!" She sold it to a fellow by the name of Lorimer who I believe was the President of American University in Washington, D.C. He owned it for several years and then sold it to Gardner Means. Gardner was a Harvard economist, class of about 1918, and became fairly well known in the 1930s and 40s because he was part of Franklin Delano Roosevelt's Brain Trust who helped plan the New Deal. I'd give $10,000 to buy Yellowhead today, without any questions asked.

The present owner has life tenancy, but happily she is leaving the island to a conservation group. I am very proud to have played a role in getting Maine started on the whole idea of conservation restrictions (more on that in the next chapter), so I am particularly glad that my favorite island will be preserved.

AVELINDA and CIRRUS rafted at Cross Island as the crews row ashore. (1950)

The beach of Northwest Cove, Cross Island, where a large salt pond drains near the location of the big lumbering camp established by Pejebscot Paper Company during the pulpwood cutting operation (1939-1942) in which 20,000 cords of wood were barged off. (1953)

* * *

My most bedeviling quest to buy property, however, was on the mainland near Haycock Harbor, where we had our cruising misadventures described in the last chapter. Haycock Harbor has a headland to the east of its entrance with a magnificent spot of luxurious ground and splendid views. Years ago it was completely primeval, and I wanted to own it. A lobsterman told me that it was owned by a man named Hurst, but he didn't know the address. I wrote to several nearby post offices, and a reply came from the postmistress at West Trescott saying that the owner was her husband. Thinking this would probably be a local fisherman, I wrote to him offering $500 for that exposed point, explaining that I was a yachtsman and had visited it. The letter in reply was pecked out on a typewriter with many corrections on a cheap piece of lined paper. It declined my offer, but seemed consistent with my assumption that he was a fisherman, so I wrote again, hoping I might be able to buy some small part of the property. The next letter I received suggested that I take my money to Wonderland and invest it in a bet on a greyhound, and maybe I might win enough money to make a real offer. Well, it took me nearly a year of correspondence before I realized that I was being led on by an expert of considerable background. I found myself razzed that I had no crew on my yacht, whereas he had had a yacht with five foremast hands. He also kidded me about my Harvard background and I felt sure he had gone to Yale. When I told him that the delay in my correspondence was caused by a month-long trip to Darjeeling in the Himalayas, he told me he had been to visit Lhasa in Tibet. By then I knew that I was up against something pretty interesting. The letters continued to be on cheap schoolblock paper and were obviously typewritten with one finger. Determined to look him up, I found that he had moved to Calais. The following summer when Virginia and I, with some friends, sailed up the St. Croix River to Calais, we went to call on Hurst. The address was a huge house left over from the days when the lumber industry brought prosperity to Calais. It was quite run down. The elaborate oaken front door had a large hasp crudely nailed on and was locked by padlock. The house was not occupied, so we had to peek in the windows under drawn shades. It was filled with books and magazines piled ceiling high. We decided to return to the village, and needing a haircut, I went into the barbershop and stated to gossip with the barber. He told me that Mr. Hurst was "a wizened up little shrimp older that Methuselah and richer than Croesus," and that he had a "five-by-five" wife.

The next letter from Hurst said that he had moved back to Trescott. We tried to find him there, but again the house was locked. We were told by neighbors that he and Mrs. Hurst were living deep in the woods east of Haycock Harbor and that the abandoned school bus in which they were living could be reached by following a swamped-out trail which Mrs. Hurst had personally cut with a chain saw. President and Mrs. Pusey of Harvard were cruising with us on *Avelinda* at the time, and needing the exercise we walked through the woods along this crude jeep trail. When we reached the school bus, we found a tiny wizened old man sitting on a stump in front of it. Although it was midsummer, he was wearing a stocking cap, two heavy overcoats, galoshes, and mitts. He was stooped forward with his chin on his chest. I introduced myself and held out my hand, but as he was getting off his glove to take it, I received a heavy push on the shoulder, and Mrs. Hurst admonished me not to touch him as it would hurt him dreadfully. She certainly had the build to both push me aside and swamp-out a road.

Hurst was delighted to meet President Pusey, and we talked of the Yale connection, which turned out to have been a correct assumption on my part. Hurst said he had been wanting to give money to Yale but didn't know where to send it, and Pusey undertook to have President Griswold of Yale write him a letter. This was the first of several talks I had with Hurst. When he died some months later I found he had left a gold pencil for me, and I was given a small lot facing the head of Haycock Harbor. Subsequently, Mrs. Hurst told me of a very bright high school boy whom she had befriended and who wanted to be a doctor. I offered to help him through Yale, but jealousy developed between the boy's mother and Mrs. Hurst, and the scholarship I had given Yale went to another Maine lad. The first boy did succeed in getting a scholarship to a less well known university, and he is now a doctor practicing in Maine.

I wish I knew more of the history of Julius Hurst, but I can only give an outline of his life. He was the scion of a prominent textile family in Lancashire, England. While he was at Harrow his parents died, and an uncle who held the purse strings tried to force him into the textile business. He went to Tasmania where he scraped up enough money to come to America and entered the medical school at Yale in 1895. Before graduating, he was accused by the dean of lying about his tardy return from a vacation in Paris and was denied a degree despite his plea of innocence. After a year at another medical school he got a residency for two years in a London hospital and finally he got an M.D. degree from Yale, but not until 1904. By then he was married and was practicing medicine in Connecticut and had a large yacht. After he lost his wife he moved to California. There, while he was driving on a country road with a girl he had picked up as a hitchhiker, the car overturned, killing her and severely injuring him. After he got out of the hospital, he decided to go to Maine to console the girl's family. While there he fell in love with the girl's younger sister who was also many years his junior. He married her and they went to live in Santa Barbara. When war broke out in 1914, he wanted to be commissioned as a doctor in the British or Canadian Army. He was rejected by both because he was underweight. Finally he got a commission in the American Army but only through the intercession of the Surgeon General. He served in field hospitals in Flanders until the war was over.

After the war he served in the Veteran's Administration until his retirement when they returned to Maine. He was badly afflicted with arthritis and was not able to hold a book or pencil, but he could peck out a letter on a typewriter. Despite his affliction, he had tremendous courage and fine sense of humor. I don't believe he weighed more than ninety pounds when he died.

* * *

A little more than ten years after my son's near-drowning at the Barred Islands, which had first stirred in me the yearning to own those islands, I learned that Butter and the two Barreds connected to it at half tide were for sale. However, the owners, George and Emory Harriman, architect brothers from Boston who had bought the islands in 1895, were asking $15,000 for the property, a price beyond my means. After they both died and the estate was finally settled, I wrote one of the daughters and was able to purchase Butter and the two connecting islets for $1,600.

For the next two to three years I tried to get the title cleared up. I never did get it entirely cleared. I hired a lawyer to study the title history, but it was useless. There were so many holes in his abstract and so many obvious contradictions that I paid him only half his usual fee. A couple in California claims to own a little over one acre on Butter, although they don't know exactly where it is.

Charles B. McLane has written in his book *Islands of the Mid-Maine Coast: Blue Hill and Penobscot Bays* about the fascinating chapter in Butter's history under the ownership of the Harriman brothers: "They conceived of Butter Island as a summer vacationland for genteel Bostonians and other pedigreed guests. Their early brochures and publicity for what they called the New England Tent Club emphasized clean, wholesome outdoor living in an 'Arabic-like town of tents and cottages.' Dogs and 'intoxicating liquors' were forbidden. The island's new name, Dirigo, after the Maine state motto, 'I lead,' was displayed in whitewashed stones on the east side. At its height, Dirigo, which was on the steamboat run from Rockland, accommodated up to 150 guests who could play tennis, swim, take long walks, and go on boat trips. Although few tents were erected, a number of large structures were built on the island, including the Casino and Club Room. After World War I, the resort declined and the buildings disappeared—entire structures were moved by boat to Deer Isle, parts of others to nearby Eagle Island, and some vanished into thin air."

One of Dirigo's features was an old farm pond which the Harrimans advertised for swimming, but which I am sure that few guests ever used. One

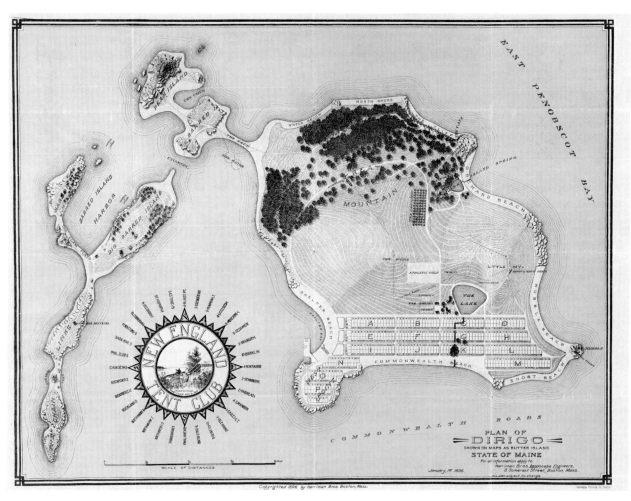

Map of the Harriman brothers' grand scheme for developing a "tent city" at Butter Island.

summer day, Virginia and I landed on Butter Island with four of our small granddaughters, the oldest of whom was eleven. We anchored at the southeast beach, our usual anchorage. Virginia and I had planned to build a trail along the south coast just inland of a swamp which is located near the south coast. We were prospecting the trail near the part of the island that is grown up from the so-called lake of Harriman's resort but which was really an old farm pond. Virginia stepped on a tuft at the marshy edge of the pond, slipped some way, and broke her leg very badly. It was clear that she had dislocated her ankle and had broken the lower end of the tibia, the weight-bearing bone of the lower leg. I was afraid she'd lose consciousness, so I laid her out as comfortably as I could and started back to the beach.

I went running through the woods, breaking branches in my way because there were no trails at all. The vessel was anchored off the beach about a half mile away and our granddaughters were playing there. When I got to the beach, I immediately organized the kids. I pulled the dinghy down to the water and sent the oldest out to *Avelinda*. I told her to get a bedsheet and some wooden sail battens and some cords. And then with the three smaller girls, I started to break trail through the dense woods so I would be able to carry Virginia out. We marked the trail so the oldest granddaughter would be able to come along the trail marked by broken branches. She caught up with us about the same time we arrived at Virginia's side. Although I couldn't reduce the fracture, with the battens and bedsheets torn in strips I tried to make Virginia's leg somewhat comfortable. I then loaded her onto my shoulders in a fireman's lift and started out for *Avelinda* with the four girls breaking branches or pulling them aside to make passage for us. In this way we got to the beach. I waded out to where the kids had prepared the dinghy and got Virginia aboard and rowed to the boat. I was able to get her up onto the deck and laid her out there. Then we proceeded at flank speed for Southwest Harbor, yelling over the VHF to the Coast Guard to have an ambulance to meet us at Southwest Harbor at Fernald's Point. It took us about two and a half hours at flank speed to reach Southwest Harbor. They had the ambulance there, and we loaded my wife onto the station wagon, mattress and all, and drove at high speed to Eastern General Hospital at Bangor where her fracture was reduced by a very skilled orthopedic surgeon.

* * *

Butter Island and the two connecting islets are among the few islands I have kept. Do I regret having given away islands that by now might be worth a good many millions of dollars? Truthfully, I am elated that I was in a position to preserve these islands, and get some tax benefits in the bargain. Butter Island and the two islets are restricted as to development and are held in a non-profit corporation. Virginia and I expect that a commemorative stone bench or other suitable memorial will be erected on the high point on the east side of the island after we are deceased. We are happy that the land will retain its current beauty for the enjoyment of our descendants and all who navigate those waters in the future.

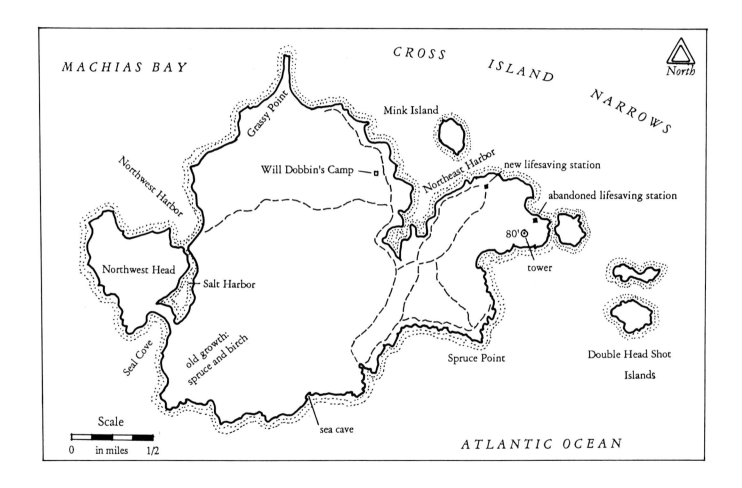

A WALK AROUND CROSS ISLAND

Most people think of the Maine islands as domes of white granite poking above the surface of the sea like so many boulders scattered on a stony New England pasture. Although this impression accurately describes the geography of a great long section of the Maine archipelago from offshore Monhegan to Beals Island near Jonesport, east of Jonesport the islands change their look. The craggy islands and the coast between Roque Island and West Quoddy Head are dominated by rocks older than the granites of the midcoast: rocks that were formed from the remnants of an age of violent volcanic explosions that made the recent eruption of Mount St. Helens look tame by comparison.

The volcanic islands and coast at the far eastern end of the Maine archipelago are not well known to most travelers because they are distant from the centers of tourism and sailing and involve long beats (or drives) back toward civilization for those who make the passage. Even if you get there, the sharp, craggy profiles and hard rock beaches don't invite you ashore as graciously as do the many pocket sand beaches between sloping granite outcrops of Maine's midcoast.

Nevertheless, the eastern islands present some of Maine's most spectacular coastal scenery and have always been more wild and untamed than other portions of the archipelago. Cross Island near the great Fundy Channel is an outpost where the geography, the deep spruce forests, and the winged, hoofed, and clawed wildlife community present a picture of what the Maine coast looked and felt like for a millennia before the first European colonizers arrived.

The best way to appreciate the variety and vastness of Cross Island's natural habitats (now part of the U.S. Fish and Wildlife National Refuge System) is to circumnavigate the island by foot hiking counterclockwise around the island starting from the abandoned red-roofed Coast Guard station on the northeast shore across from Mink Island. Because the huge tidal currents surge back and forth between the shores of Cross and Mink Islands, marine wildlife congregates here in large numbers. More often than not a bald eagle or two are perched in the highest peaks of the spruce trees on Mink Island waiting for the tidal conveyer belt to present a meal.

Just beyond the first headland, west of the Coast Guard Station, Northeast Harbor cuts deeply into the interior of Cross Island diverting a hiker far from the northern rim of the island in order to cross a stream and wetland that feeds into the cove from Cross' forested interior. The huge mudflats of Northeast Harbor at low tide are full of marine life including extensive beds of soft-shelled clams and blue mussels around the edges of seaweed choked tidepools. Around the next headland to the westward is a small unnamed cove where Will Dobbins' fishing camp was located and where old logging roads, now almost completely grown up, came down off the high ground to access the large tracts of spruce forest that extend across a thousand acres of the interior. The shores of this cove are lined with raspberry and rose bushes, and the shingle beach is covered by dense mats of beach pea above the high water mark.

By keeping to the shoreline and crossing over craggy volcanic outcrops and other small unnamed beaches, you find yourself looking out at a long, low, narrow finger of land that trends out toward Cross Island Narrows. Called Grassy Point after the hardy northern and Arctic grasses that cover its rocky underpinnings, this little piece of boreal habitat is much more common to the Coast of Labrador than to the Maine coast. At the extreme seaward end of Grassy Point at low tide are extensive tide pools filled with sea anemones, large moon snails, and a variety of sea stars and other marine life common to shores of much more northern latitudes.

After a succession of numerous additional nameless beaches and headlands, you finally come to the edge of beautiful Northwest Harbor, which is rimmed by large, steep shingle beaches piled up by winter's northwesterly gales. Behind the beach a very large saltmarsh is spread between the massive headlands of Cross Island proper and Northwest Head, a hundred-acre peninsula on Cross' western flank. This salt marsh, which sustains large numbers of migratory waterfowl, especially Arctic nesting shorebirds on their way south, nearly cuts the westernmost part of Cross Island in two.

If you keep to the eastern shore near the southern end of the salt marsh and then ascend the southwest sloping hillside, you come into stands of old growth red spruce and yellow birch that have never been lumbered. These woodlands on Cross' western edge form a virtually undisturbed natural community; you are privileged to be seeing a biological community that is essentially identical to the coast of Maine as described by Champlain, Waymouth, and Captain John Smith almost four hundred years

earlier. It is this habitat where a pair of bald eagles have maintained a nest site for the past decade. Further inland, around the edges of streams, wetlands, and waterholes, you may find the tracks of black bear. Bears need large individual ranges, and Cross probably does not support more than a few. Once widely distributed from Mexico to the Arctic Circle, black bears are now confined primarily to wild mountain areas. Maine supports the East's largest bear population, but most of them are found in the northern Maine woods. Black bears are omnivorous, feeding on a great variety of fruits, nuts, seeds, roots, green plants, insects, rodents, fish, carrion, and the young of wild ungulates (deer). Probably as a result of the bear (and incidentally, also raccoon and coyote), seabirds do not nest in any numbers on Cross. Raccoons, in particular, prey on the eggs and young of waterfowl. Most of the area's interesting bird life nests on the small, nearby islands.

It is another half hour hike south along the shores of Seal Cove where both harbor and gray seals crawl out on ledges to rest and feed their pups in the early summer. Having made it this far along Cross' extensive, endlessly diverse inner shores, you have probably spent close to six hours of hiking, and are ready for the most spectacular part of Cross' scenic ecology: its outer shores.

The topography of the southern coast is by far the most rugged and forbidding of any large Maine island. It is more closely related to endless miles of the Labrador coast than any other place along the Maine coast. The bedrock is composed of tightly fractured, brittle, needle-shaped volcanic rocks that have eroded in sharp, jagged pieces. The fracture planes in the bedrock are bent and swirled in a frozen testament of the uneasy movement of the earth's crust over eons of time. These ancient rocks have been cut by numerous small intrusions of other rock units from later episodes of volcanic activity. Here and there old dikes of frozen lava have been eroded away leaving narrow, vertical-walled crevices which makes progress on foot slow but interesting. Along the central portion of the southern coast is a small rock arch just big enough to crawl through. It appears to have been formed when a quartz and feldspar vein created a weakened zone in the surrounding rock which erosional forces have differentially affected.

As you proceed east along Cross' southern shore, before the last major headland is reached, the color of the bedrock changes abruptly from dark gray-greens to yellow-purple hues of an ancient volcanic sedimentary unit. In a narrow little bight that is easy to miss if you're in too much of a hurry, is a small beach not thirty feet across. At the head of the beach is a beautiful, eery, seventy-foot long sea cave whose entrance is covered at high water. This cave is a product of the same processes which formed Anemone Cave on Mount Desert and the sea cave on Bald Porcupine Island in Frenchman's Bay. Here an erodible sedimentary unit is capped by a resistant sheet of massive igneous rock. The waves act differently on the two units, successfully attacking the weaker, eventually channeling greater and greater amounts of energy at the point of indentation so that over geologic time, the force of the sea is able to quarry out the softer rock to sculpt the beautiful cave.

By the time you've reached Spruce Point, the last major headland on the southern shore, you will probably need a rest. This headland is a good a place along this outermost shore to watch for whales—particularly right whales, which frequently cruise right up underneath Cross' cliffs in one hundred feet of water to feed on the legendary schools of herring that come inshore to spawn and feed every summer.

Finally, after passing along the cut that separates Scotch Island from Cross itself, you come into the last cove and beach where the old life-saving station is slowly moldering away on a beach reshaped by northeasterly gales many times since it was originally constructed.

By circumnavigating Cross Island you will have cut across almost a dozen eco-types or habitats from rocky headland to shingle beach, from boreal tidepool to salt marsh and from old growth forest to quaking bog. In the process, you will have sampled a great number of the habitats across the length and breadth of Maine. In this sense, you will have seen Maine in a microcosm, which will continue to remain as wild as the day you found it due to the vision of a man who first saw it over sixty years ago and wanted to protect it forever.

Unusual stop seine barge for catching herring in small coves in Nova Scotia. (1948)

CHAPTER 6

*C*onserving the Coast

One Evening At A Cocktail Party On Mount Desert Island In About 1960, Peggy Rockefeller, the wife of banker David Rockefeller, asked me if I would sell her one of my islands. She thought I owned half the islands on the Maine coast, which, of course, was an exaggeration. I told her that I would be happy to undertake to buy her an island instead. I mentioned that I had, in fact, that very day in Buckle Harbor on Swans Island met a fisherman, Carl Lawson, who offered to sell me his house when I had asked him who owned the land we had been walking through on the north shore. I didn't want the house, but he also owned about eighty acres on Swans Island, the whole of Buckle Island, which formed the other side of the harbor, and several little islets. A real estate person had told him he ought to get about $4,500 for the house and land. I said I was very interested but I didn't have the time to discuss it with him then because I had left guests on my yacht, which was anchored in Scallop Cove. I told Peggy about Buckle Island at the cocktail party, thinking it might be appropriate for her, and she persuaded me to give her Lawson's name. I mentioned that I would be heading out there again early in the morning.

Apparently, she lay awake that night dreaming about this island, and finally got up at three a.m. to sail her little boat, *Jack Tar*, which had no engine, to Buckle Harbor, where she joined my conversation with Lawson. She offered him $800 for Buckle Island, but he said he had promised it to me and didn't want to discuss the sale of Buckle as a separate transaction. She persisted, but he finally told her he wasn't sure whether he had title to all of the island. He thought he had at least a four-fifths undivided interest in the island. A great deal of land in Maine is held as undivided portions of a total ownership, which have been handed down over the generations and get fractionally smaller over time. Peggy became concerned as to whether he could give good title. She told him that she would be back and went off to consult with her lawyer.

About three or four days later I arrived in Buckle Harbor in *Avelinda*, went ashore, and offered Lawson a better deal than $4,500. Namely, I said that I would buy the house and lands, including the islands, for $3,900 in cash and would give him a lease back for a minimum of three years free. Because the taxes were $220 per year, he would be better off under that deal than selling me the house outright at $4,500. He accepted the deal and I asked for a piece of paper so we could write out the agreement. He didn't have paper or pencil, so I went out to the vessel to get them and wrote out a little agreement. While I was doing so, into the harbor came the *Jack Tar*, the Rockefeller yacht, with Peggy aboard. She had a document with a blue backing and red seals all prepared by the lawyer. I suggested that we go ashore together, which we did.

Lawson's son protested that I was cheating his father and that the property was worth at least $6,000. He said he had received an offer of $6,000 for the property that very afternoon. I knew he had been out lobster fishing all that afternoon, so I replied, "If you can get $6,000 for it, go ahead," and started to walk away. At this point his father called after me, "But Mr. Cabot, we had a deal that you would buy the property for $3,900 with a three-year free lease." "Yes, that's so." "Well, did you make the document for me?" "Yes," and I took the document out of my pocket with a dollar bill in it for his consideration. I volunteered that Mrs. Rockefeller also had a document prepared by her lawyer, at which point the son began to yell, "Mrs. Rockefeller?" He was very excited because previously we hadn't revealed who she was. But his father was as good as his word. He put his name on my paper, with Peggy as witness, and that was the deal. Then he said, "I'll sign the other document, too." So he put his name on Peggy's six pages, which I hadn't read. It took us no more than about three days to examine the title for the entire property, whereupon Peggy received her title to Buckle Island for $800. However, it was only good with respect to four-fifths undivided interest. She had to pay another $500 to get the full title and get it recorded.

With the help of two of her daughters, Peggy built a cabin on Buckle Island with her own hands. Later, the Rockefellers bought a much larger island west of Mount Desert, which had a few old farm buildings on it that they rebuilt. Peggy drove a huge bulldozer herself to restore the open pastures for her herd of registered cattle. A World War II surplus landing craft brings the cattle back and forth across from the mainland.

In order to preserve more islands, Peggy and her banker husband, David, began buying other islands such as a large part of Frenchboro, Long Island, off Mount Desert, and Foster Island in Narraguagus Bay. In about 1965 she came to me to ask what we could do to save the rest of the Maine coast. I told her, "You can't save it all by buying it. That would be too expensive—even for the Rockefellers." I suggested a better scheme, which was to persuade owners of uninhabited islands and some of the headlands to put scenic restrictions on them.

The concept of restrictions was not new. The Conservation Foundation in Washington, D.C., which was formed in the 1930s, was probably the first organization to propose such a scheme. One of the earliest conservation philanthropies in the world in which I played a small part is The Trustees of Reservations in Massachusetts, founded in 1891 in Boston, which has protected a great deal of significant lands throughout the Commonwealth of Massachusetts. It was the forerunner of the National Trusts of England, Scotland, and Ireland, after which these agencies were modeled. The Trustees of Reservations was founded a hundred years ago by the son of Charles William Eliot, President of Harvard. He was a protégé of Frederic Law Olmstead, the great landscape architect who designed Central Park in New York City and a beautiful property known as World's End on a point of land at the southern end of Boston Harbor. I was very familiar with their conservation work in Massachusetts and wanted to help get a conservation program started in Maine.

* * *

At this time I became concerned about the environment through the writings of Rachel Carson who described how the songs of the birds were disappearing from the accumulation of pesticides in the food chain. She was very eloquent about it, and she convinced a good friend of mine by the name of Dennis

Osprey nest, Barred Islands. (1954)

Puleston, an English trained Ph. D. in organismic biology, to devote his life to saving birds and saving the primeval quality of the habitat of the birds. Puleston is a hero of mine because he was the one who got the first law passed banning DDT, initially in New York and then nationally. Every one of our conservation societies owes a real debt to these two people for focusing public concern on the destruction of the primeval quality of the world. Rachel Carson was a poet, if you like, who alerted people to what they were losing; Puleston was the scientist who got laws passed. Of course, the whole movement against the destruction of the primeval quality of the habitat is now on almost everyone's mind, particularly the problems of the pollution of the atmosphere and the pollution of the oceans.

* * *

These thoughts were in my mind as Peggy Rockefeller and I began to discuss what we might be able to do to preserve primeval habitat along the Maine coast. After I had broached the concept of conservation easements with Peggy, she consulted a private law firm, Millbank, Tweed, Hadley & McCoy, who appointed a young Harvard law graduate by the name of Dave Strawbridge to investigate this idea. Strawbridge called me by phone and I explained that you could get conservation restrictions put on the land by selling the land to a third person who then would deed it back with the restrictions on it. He replied that such a process seemed pretty cumbersome, and believed it would be more useful to get a law passed so the restrictions could be put on land directly. Along with Robert Patterson, one of the founders of the Natural Resources Council of Maine and a state legislator, they were instrumental

From Acadia Mountain looking into Somes Sound, the only true fiord on the Atlantic coast of the United States. (1949)

in getting a bill passed in the Maine legislature authorizing the use of conservation easements. Subsequently in 1970, the Maine Coast Heritage Trust was formed to promote the idea of easements among coastal landowners. Peggy was the first president, but soon Harold E. Woodsum, a partner in one of Portland's leading law firms became president and I was vice-president.

A private, non-profit organization, Maine Coast Heritage Trust has as its purpose to protect land for scenic, recreational, agricultural, and other reasons. A working fishing harbor, for example, can be considered as significant a treasure as a dramatic headland. The Maine Coast Heritage Trust is now a flourishing organization with a professional staff skilled in different aspects of land conservation. Some 47,000 acres and 147 entire islands on the Maine coast have been preserved to date by the Trust, which has cooperated with many other institutions, including The Nature Conservancy and the Maine and National Audubon Societies, as well as the Department of Inland Fisheries and Wildlife and Acadia National Park. Since 1987 the Maine Coast Heritage Trust has promoted the formation of local land trusts; there are now more than sixty such trusts just in Maine, which oversee about 11,000 acres of protected private land. One of the previous Executive Directors of Maine Coast Heritage Trust, Benjamin Emory, was the head of the Land Trust Alliance, the umbrella organization for the land trust movement all around the United States. Emory lives on Mount Desert Island and is very active in promoting land trusts, not only around the country but around the world. If the people of a local community become interested in preserving land, they often know better than outsiders what land should be preserved and what should be developed.

Lunt Harbor, Frenchboro. (1964)

In purely practical terms, conservation easements offer many advantages to landowners. The owners are free to tailor easements to their own needs, restricting part or all of their land, as they wish. They can retain the title and sole right of access to their land, if they wish. They pay taxes only on the remainder value, not on the development value, which may be about eighty percent of the total, an important factor with regard to estate taxes. If the public benefits from the restriction, there may in addition be a charitable deduction.

For small towns, studies have shown that the annual local tax reduction may in fact be less than the added cost to the town of the additional services caused by development. When a town develops land, the tax base is increased, which is good for the town in the short run, but the town has to build schools, roads, enlarge the police force, and so forth, which can be expensive in the long run. The tax rate has to go up faster than the growth in population to support all these services.

* * *

On occasion, the battle to preserve the primeval character of the Maine coast had taken me into the courtroom as well. In the early 1970s, the Occidental Petroleum Company wanted to build a so-called oil refinery on Machias Bay across from Cross Island and near Yellow Head. I knew that Bruce Sprague, a native Mainer who owned a big piece of land where a pipeline was supposed to go ashore on the Point of Main, was offered a substantial price for his land, but he declined to sell it to Armand Hammer, the president of Occidental. I joined other conservationists in opposing the refinery not only because it would have been an eyesore on that primeval shore, but because it

Rowing against the tide trying to get into the Basin on Vinalhaven's western shores. (1939)

would have been an economic boondoggle as well. The proposal was to create a free port sponsored by the State of Maine, which would condemn enough land to cover the needs of the refinery and ancillary industries, as well as building a 1,500-foot dock on the exposed side of Stone Island, at the entrance of picturesque Starboard Harbor. My opposition was due not just to the impairment of the scenic beauty of that part of the coast, but also because the proposal was grossly unfair to other processors of crude oil and semi-refined products, including Cabot Corporation. At that time, oil imports were restricted by quota, and Occidental was asking for such a disproportionate quota that it would have profited about 100 percent per year on its investment from the quota alone.

At the hearing on the proposal at the Federal Court House in Portland, Occidental was represented by Louis Nizer, the famous trial lawyer from New York. I had driven to Portland from Boston and when I arrived, I found there was such a large crowd around the courthouse entrance, it would be difficult to get in. I knew most of the oil men who were gathered outside because I was in the petrochemical business, and they were all trying to decide who would go first in opposing this project. They urged me to speak first and started pushing me ahead when I ran into a fellow by the name of Frank Coffin who was one of the top federal judges. He has since become the chief judge of the First Circuit Court in the First District, and he asked me what I was doing there. I said I was going to testify, but I couldn't get in. He told me to follow him, and I was able to get into the courthouse through his private quarters. He suggested I go sit in the jurors' box. "That way you'll have the best seat in the place."

About the time the hearing started and I was getting ready to testify, Hale Boggs, a Congressman from Louisiana, came up to me and said, "Do you mind if I go ahead of you? I've got to get back to Washington because they're going to have a vote and I've got a plane standing by." I told him to be my guest. Boggs asked Nizer why Occidental had to hire a New Yorker at $10,000 per day when there were plenty of Maine lawyers who could do the job for much less and who were reputed to be the smartest in the nation. He then said he came to Maine to testify because Occidental had offered him $100,000 for his support. He said, "You can't bribe me; I've got to protect my reputation." He put on a marvelous display of righteousness.

My testimony came next and caught Nizer's expert witnesses by surprise because they found me not only a yachtsman and conservationist, but as experienced in fleet operations as his experts. For several years formerly I had been president of United Fruit Company whose Great White Fleet contained a hundred ships. It was the greatest tourist fleet in the world, and I spoke in detail concerning the difficulties of successfully managing the navigation of the fleet of tankers that would be coming in and out of Machias Bay. The application was denied. This segment of the Maine coast is now mostly covered by scenic easements given by Bruce Sprague and other sympathetic owners that will protect its primeval character in perpetuity.

* * *

The Maine coast is subject to many pressures and uncertainties, overpopulation and the attendant forces of development, among them. I have been active for forty years in trying to prevent overpopulation in the world, but with discouragingly little success. When I began trying to prevent overpopulation in the world, I had great hopes that we would stabilize the population in about twenty-five years. I'm sorry to say that we have made very little progress toward stabilizing population and it is getting more and more difficult to justify the millions of dollars that I and friends have put into the population problem. As long as the population grows, land will have to be developed, and we're going to use every acre of land to produce enough food for places that have just enough room to put up houses. Given this fact, the problem is to keep development from destroying all the primeval land. I believe the loss of primeval land will tragically impair our quality of life and irrevocably damage that of our descendants.

In the face of the many uncertainties facing the Maine coast, I have tried to save what I can. I have given away almost all of the forty-one islands I originally purchased, either to The Nature Conservancy for transfer with restrictions to the Department of the Interior, or to the State of Maine. The Nature Conservancy is a wonderful organization. I have dealt with them in four different states where I have helped protect land—Maine, New Hampshire, Massachusetts, and Colorado. They're very active in all the states in the country and have been extremely effective in getting philanthropic money channeled into conservation.

In 1983 I decided that the restrictions I had put on Cross Island were not enough to protect it and the nearby islets and that I would better give them away as well. I had already donated about thirty acres on Cross to the Hurricane Island Outward Bound School. For more than three years I tried to give the group of islands to the federal government. The Fish and Wildlife Service of the Department of the Interior was interested, but they fussed around and couldn't tell me whether or not they could accept the islands as a gift. Finally, I happened to sit next to the Secretary of the Interior during a dinner at the Kennedy School at Harvard. I told him that for three years I had been trying to give him $1 million worth of islands. The Secretary said, "I'll get you an answer by next Monday." Three to four months later, I got his answer that the United States Fish and Wildlife Service would accept the islands. Now fully protected, they are at the western end of the spectacular thirty-five-mile stretch of Bold Coast extending east to Quoddy Head, along which the Maine Coast Heritage Trust has recently been helping acquire important headlands for protection.

* * *

The only islands I still keep in the family are Butter Island and the two connecting islets, but I have put conservation easements on them. In fact, the first conservation easement in Maine was the one I wrote for Butter.

Butter Island is a good example of the kinds of dilemmas confronting the Maine islands. Today, about four thousand people visit Butter annually, so some kind of control is needed to prevent irreparable damage to the fragile environment. Butter Island was farmed until 1930 or thereabouts. The last farmhouse burned down in about 1932. We have pictures of Butter Island as it was eighty or ninety years ago showing several farm houses on it when most of the island was bare. It had been used as pasture. The famous "lake" is now just a tangle of bushes. The whole island is reverting to a wild state. Although it obviously would be a tragedy if our nation no longer had any primeval land, how much of what kinds of wilderness do we need? The idea of a wilderness into which you can get by foot, on boat, on skiis, or horseback, I think is a good idea. I'm for it. But it's very difficult to find a good compromise between pure wilderness where nobody can visit or use and undeveloped multi-use lands. I believe only small portions of land should be so set aside that can be visited only by scientists who are trying to see what the land would be like with no human influence on that land. I would argue that the amount of wilderness that has been set out as wilderness under the federal laws is much larger than needed just to see what an undisturbed land would be like. I think that land should be available for access by people who come in such a way that they're not destroying the wildlife or changing it very substantially, visually or otherwise.

On Butter Island, with all the use it receives, a caretaker is necessary to keep people from building fires, which might spread, and from leaving trash; written permission is needed to camp. My family maintains the pasture by cutting trees on it (otherwise tree-cutting is not allowed on the island) and by introducing sheep. It is a fallacy to think that all islands should be left to grow back to their wild state. Maintenance is required to keep open areas for their scenic beauty and for access.

I maintain the trails, which are nevertheless wearing out and may need stone steps. But it is a difficult compromise to make—between maintaining Butter in an aesthetically attractive condition and allowing the public to enjoy it thus. I don't know what Butter Island will be like in fifty to one hundred years, but I am trying to conserve it so that it will be a beautiful island forever and not selfishly restrict all access to its stunning features.

One year in the recent past we had about nine different outfits wanting to bring big groups onto Butter Island. It became obvious that we were going

Butter Island trail blazing. (1943)

to have to limit use, which is why I have become interested in the Maine Island Trail concept of the Island Institute, in which those who use the islands for recreation assume responsibility for their stewardship. It is now our policy to restrict overnight use to members of the Island Trail Association. That has limited several problems, but by no means eliminated all. One day several years ago, I came into Barred Island Harbor and could see there was a big tent on the shore of Butter Island. It was dusk and I thought I ought to tell those people they had no permission to pitch a tent there. But I was in a hurry to anchor and get dinner so I didn't. The next morning I rowed over, around 7 o'clock, to the beach where the tent was pitched. As I approached, a man and his wife came down to the beach, and before I had even gotten ashore, he hailed me with a hearty, "Welcome to the 'Beggar on Horseback!'" referring to the title of my autobiography. Of course, I tried to be polite to him, but I told him he should have gotten written permission. He said he would next time. I found out that he was a physician and one of the top doctors at Eastern Maine Medical Hospital in Bangor. His wife was also a physician there. Because I have devoted a good deal of my life to medical economics and served as trustee of various medical boards we had a lot to talk about, so I couldn't really be angry with him.

The Maine Island Trail concept is quite new—developed in the late 1980s by David R. Getchell, Sr., of the Island Institute, with its pilot season only in 1989—but it offers a provocative alternative to protection through outright ownership or scenic easements: protection through user-based stewardship. Some 2,200 people have already joined the organization, many of them kayakers, but representing all varieties of small boat ownership. For an annual membership fee, they receive a detailed guidebook and permission to camp on state-owned and specifically designated privately owned islands. In return, members serve as a stewardship presence on the uninhabited islands, cleaning up after themselves and others, monitoring use patterns, and setting a good example of island use by demonstrating low-impact camping techniques. It's too soon to know how it will work out, but it's an effort to try to create the kind of balance that I hope we can maintain on the Maine coast, and I have been happy to let the Island Trail use Butter Island as a kind of guinea pig.

Maine Coast Heritage Trust: Two Decades of Successful Conservation

The Maine Coast Heritage Trust is a land trust, that is, a private non-profit organization whose purpose is the protection of land for scenic, agricultural, recreational, or other purposes. Its special mission is "to protect land that is essential to the character of Maine, its coastline and islands in particular."

Although it has protected some 47,000 acres and 147 islands in their entirety in its twenty-year history in the state, it actually owns relatively few of these acres and islands, relying instead on the imaginative use of a legal device called the conservation easement. Indeed, the easement played a key role in the founding of the Trust.

The inspiration that grew into the Maine Coast Heritage Trust struck Peggy Rockefeller in 1970 when she and her husband, banker David Rockefeller, were cruising off Stonington and noticed that an island that had been free of development the year before now had four or five houses crowding the shoreline.

She then consulted with friends—among them Tom Cabot and family attorney Don O'Brien—about the threat she perceived, and the strategy they suggested was using conservation easements to protect Maine's coastal islands. Robert Patterson, one of the founders of the Natural Resources Council of Maine and a state legislator at the time, introduced a bill authorizing the use of conservation easements and worked successfully for its passage. With this tool at their disposal Cabot and the Rockefellers then went ahead to form the Maine Coast Heritage Trust in order to promote the easement concept among the owners

of coastal property. The Trust's founders realized that with ninety-six percent of the Maine Coast in private hands, private conservation initiatives would be crucial in preserving it.

In the organization's early years, when the Trust focused its efforts almost entirely on protecting islands in Penobscot Bay and near Acadia National Park, the park became the major holder of the easements that Maine Coast Heritage Trust negotiated. As the Trust expanded its work up and down the coast, it began to arrange gifts and sales of land as well as donations of easements to many other private and public holders, such as The Nature Conservancy, National Audubon Society, the Department of Inland Fisheries and Wildlife, towns, and local land trusts.

Not only did the Maine Coast Heritage Trust lead the way in the easement's use as a tool for land conservation, it also was among the first to spring to its defense in 1980 when pending changes in federal tax law threatened the deductibility of easements. "That threat brought land trusts from all over the country together," recalls Ben Emery, executive director of the Trust from 1976 to 1982. These increased contacts led to the formation of the Land Trust Exchange (recently renamed the Land Trust Alliance), a national organization to provide information and assistance to land trusts throughout the country and to represent them in Washington. Emery served as its first director.

In recent years the Trust's most spectacular efforts have been directed toward Washington County's "Bold Coast," the thirty-five-mile stretch from Western Head to the Canadian border rep-

resenting the last wild section of the Maine coast. The acquisition and protection of Western Head, Great Head, and Boot Head in 1988 was a conservation triumph that any organization could be proud of, but Maine Coast Heritage Trust did not stop there. In 1989 it put together a public and private partnership to acquire the 11,000-acre Hearst Corporation lands in Cutler and neighboring Whiting. The 2,100-acre section of this property, purchased for the state under the Land for Maine's Future program, includes four-and-one half miles of spectacular coastline. The "backland" section was purchased by the Conservation Fund, a private nationwide land-conservation organization, which is leasing these lands to Maine Coast Heritage Trust to manage for wildlife-habitat protection, traditional public uses, and timber production.

Clearly, one of the major factors in Maine Coast Heritage Trust's success has been its focus. The emotional impetus that called the Trust into being was a love for the Maine coast, and though it has expanded its scope over the past 20 years, both in terms of its geographic area and activities, it has never spread its resources too thin, and the Maine coast and its islands still remain its top priority. But now, going into its third decade, the Maine Coast Heritage Trust is busier than ever. The development threat to the Maine coast has not abated, and the Trust finds itself increasingly in demand to help protect not just the scenic beauty of Maine but its working resources and its way of life, both on the coast and inland.

The photographs of Swans Island people in this chapter were generously lent by Mary Mohler and present scenes of island life during the past century. The scene above was taken in the 1890s at Garden Point which is now the location of Tom and Virginia's house.

CHAPTER 7

*S*wallowing the Anchor

WHEN OLD AGE MADE US UNABLE TO SPEND OUR SUMMERS CRUISING, Virginia and I decided to build a summer home on Swans Island, six miles off-shore from Mount Desert. The island was named for Colonel James Swan of Boston who bought it as a land speculator in 1786. He was a worldly man of considerable wealth who refused to pay a dubious French debt and spent many years in debtor's prison in Paris. The first settlement on Swans was in the southwest part of the island near Irish Point where there is a good anchorage and some of the best arable land. Today there are only cellar holes left.

We have always liked Swans Island because it has not yet become exclusively a summer colony, and we still like it because of the islanders' friendliness and hospitality. We built on a lovely point of land far from the main village and far from the ferry wharf. Our house is on Garden Point, on the northwest tip of the island. It was cleared for farming at about the beginning of the nineteenth century and was pasture land for over one hundred years. The land looks across several channels of deep water through which the tide floods and ebbs and from which we see dozens of wooded islands with high rocky bluffs. It is one of the loveliest places on the coast. We are in a grove of red oak, huge trees that are more than two centuries old, with young spruce, birch, and poplar growing among them. The sailing yachts and fishing boats pass near to the shore through the channels, which for millennia were used by the Indians in their canoes of white birchbark. The beach of clam shells is evidence of how long Indians camped on our point to feast on shellfish from the coves on either side of the point.

When we were still contemplating the construction of the first summer house we had ever had on the Maine coast, I had an unsettling experience on the land in which we were to build. I was cruising with a couple and there were just the three of us aboard *Avelinda*. They were the kind of people who didn't like to walk. We stopped in Buckle Harbor on July 19, 1983. I wanted some exercise; they didn't. So I left them smoking cigarettes in the harbor and rowed ashore. I walked up to the house to call on Dorothy Killam who had been bedridden and lived all alone. She's still alive and in a nursing home, but at that time she still lived on the island. It's about a mile up to her house from the harbor and it's nearly two miles from her house to Garden Point.

In the course of our conversation, I said to her that there seemed to be a lot of traffic on the road in front of her house. She said, "Yes, they're extending it down to Garden Cove." I said, "Down to Garden Cove? What are they doing that for?" "I don't know," she said, "but I know they tell me it goes down toward Garden Cove." So I decided to see where this road went. I walked for what seemed like three or four miles, but actually it was only about a mile and three-quarters. I was in the woods all the way and hadn't been particularly keeping track of the the direction. I was puzzled about the whole thing and still wondering where it was going and thinking about the guests I had left out on the boat when I saw some fellows ahead and hurried toward them. They were surveyors and I asked them what they were doing, but before they could answer I realized they were on my land. When I told them where they were, they made no denial. They only told me they were surveying for a land owner whose land was adjacent to mine on the inner shores of Garden Cove. Although he had gotten ahold of the property for almost nothing, he was now asking $350,000 for it. I had tried to buy a piece from him some twenty years before, but he wouldn't sell it then. I was upset that he would build a road across my property without my permission, so I called him up about it. He said he thought he was doing me a favor. He told me, "I'm building a road so you can get into your back land without having to pay for a road to do it. It's going to be a public road, and you can have right of way on it." I replied that I didn't want a right of way on it; that I came there for solitude. I also said that he obviously had the right to go and build on his side of the point if he wanted to, but he would have to get there by water, not by land. After protracted legal proceedings, I was finally able to buy him out, although I was forced to pay him more than I thought the land was worth.

* * *

With our privacy thus ensured, the building project got underway in the late fall of 1983. I designed the house myself, using as a basis a plan I bought, but I altered the house from the original plan to such an extent that a fully new bill of materials was required. The materials were shipped in one freight car to Bangor, where they were loaded onto two trucks which brought them out onto the island. Two months were required to build the road to the house site, so the trucks weren't able to deliver the building materials until January 1984.

We started digging the cellar hole before the frost was deep in the ground. The house was finished in about four months' time from the completion of the foundation and we moved in before the end of May in 1984. We were able to complete the house rapidly because we hired everybody we could find on Swans Island who wanted to work. Nearly every fisherman is pretty good with a hammer and saw. We had a boss carpenter. All hands were paid the same wage whether a skilled laborer or someone unemployed, and I paid the bills directly to the workers. I had no superintendent, no contractor, and no architect, but it's a house of which I'm very proud. I built the house on Swans Island more than one hundred feet from the shore and couldn't put it back much farther because of wetlands. I was very careful to leave a fringe of trees. We can see through the trees to get small vistas, but as you come past our house on a boat you can hardly see it.

* * *

The Puritan work ethic is still strong on Swans Island and there is a tradition of cooperation and mutual respect among the islanders. The selectmen are all fishermen, and the island is by and for the year-round residents. There is more honesty and less violence here than we have found elsewhere. There may be less concern with world affairs and foreign cultures than in the university centers where we have mostly lived, but a fair number of retired professors, preachers, artists, and research scientists live on the island who have seen much of the world.

I respect the people of Swans Island as hardworking people who cope with all the things that need to be dealt with when you live on an island. Islanders are especially independent. Isolation develops special skills in people, and islanders have adapted admirably to the lack of available services. You can't hire people to come in and fix your plumbing every day; you've got to be able to do things for yourself. Islanders need to be jacks-of-all-trades and most of them are. It is much more difficult for Maine islanders to attend high school than for urban dwellers on the mainland, but they learn by doing things and have many more skills than most city people. Those islanders who move ashore usually fare well in competition with urbanites.

I've worked alongside of Swans Islanders, and they had skills that I didn't have, but I had some skills they didn't have. I think the best compliment I've had in recent years came from a Swans Island resident who said when the subject of Tom Cabot came up, "Oh, he's just plain as dirt." That's a real compliment, because what is meant is that people don't think of me as a snob. Everybody on Swans Island uses his or her first name. They don't call any fellow out there mister, least of all me. I'm just Tom; I'm "old Tom," I guess, to most of them.

We've had our trying moments, of course. One of the most difficult standoffs was my run-in with the Swans Island Electrical Co-op, although by

Turn of the century sailing party aboard a fishing vessel off Swans Island.

now it's become one of my favorite stories on myself. Bringing power down to Garden Point would necessitate more than two miles of underground cable, and to economize as much as possible, I searched around the country and turned up a good bargain on several spools of aluminum cable. But the Co-op manager, David Honey, refused to hook them up, following the entrenched local wisdom on the subject that aluminum cable is subject to corrosion in the island's iron-rich soil.

It got to be an awful row. I threatened David Honey with legal action; I promised to take him all the way to the Supreme Court. Honey just stood there, and all he had to say was, "And *when* did you say you wanted your electricity, Mr. Cabot?"

That old Yankee had me over a barrel, and he knew it. One of the things I most respect about Swans Islanders is that nobody—including Tom Cabot—is going to tell them how to run their business.

* * *

The internal combustion engine and the black-topped highway have made the Maine coast easily accessible and no longer mysterious in recent years. The solitude of the eastern coast is fast disappearing. Among the smaller islands, the farms have mostly gone, the quarries and boatyards have closed, and many of the fisheries have been abandoned. The summer population of the larger islands, especially those served by ferry, is increasing, but the permanent population on most of the larger islands has declined.

The islands have gone from cod fishing, to growing wheat, to pasture farming, to quarrying, to lobstering, and now to salmon farming and catering

Aerial view of Burnt Cove Harbor, Swans Island. (Photograph by Robert Hylander)

Swans Island Through Good Times and Bad

It was 1786 when the freewheeling Colonel James Swan, a minor Revolutionary War hero, obtained from the state of Massachusetts a deed for "Burnt Coat Island" (soon to be renamed) and set about building his own island empire which included a lumber mill, a grist mill, and a baronial estate overlooking the harbor. Swan's spurt of activity was short-lived. His entrepreneurial wheelings and dealings landed him in debtor's prison in France, and his mansion was soon claimed, via squatter's rights, by one David Smith who had moved into the area from New Hampshire. Smith approached the matter of settlement in a more traditional manner. He produced children—some twenty of them, for which he still bears the local nickname "King David"—and the children stayed to farm and fish.

Throughout most of the nineteenth century, Swans Island was remote, but hardly more so than any other place; in fact, in an era when the major highways were by sea rather than by land, it was a good deal more central than some. By the late nineteenth century the island's fortunes were on the upswing. Its mackerel fishermen were legendary along the coast, with Captain Herman Joyce and his schooner ALICE leading the entire New England fleet in catches. Soon afterwards islanders discovered yet another cash crop—lobsters, so plentiful they could be plucked right off the shoreline—and fortunes soared still higher.

By the turn of the century, Swans Island's population had peaked at about eight hundred. Three fish processing plants added a second thriving industry to the already flourishing fishing, while on the east side of the harbor a stone quarry was going

full tilt, providing paving blocks for what local pride still remembers as "half the streets of New York." The steamboat made regular stops, and a lively tourist industry announced its presence by a huge hotel at the head of the Steamboat Wharf Road.

But with a closer connection to the mainland came a greater dependency as well, and as the nation's economic tide turned, Swans Island's prosperity slowly ebbed. The quarry halted operations in the late 1920s, and the fish plants folded one by one as Swans Island, like the rest of the nation, entered the Depression. The population steadily dwindled, and as economic contact with the mainland faded away, the island was left to its own devices. Then in 1942 the government commandeered Swans Island's beloved steamboat for wartime purposes, and the island was plunged into isolation.

That period is remembered well by most of the island's "over forty" population, who recall the struggle with poverty, combined with a plucky self-sufficiency and a deep sense of community. "Everybody was the same poor, so it didn't seem so bad," one island woman remembers. "Besides, there were more berries than you could bake into pies, and more fish cakes than your stomach could hold."

The turnaround began shortly after World War II. By the late 1940s rural electrification loans were bringing power to the islands, and Swans selectmen, with considerable hustling, managed to get their island aboard. The lines were strung in 1950, and Swans wasted little time catching up with the rest of the world. According to island biographer Perry Westbrook, in one year (1953) islanders spent roughly $59,000 equipping their *homes with artesian wells, indoor plumbing, and some thirty vacuum cleaners and sixty-five television sets. And by the end of the decade the biggest move of all was underway. Swans watched for a while as the other islands started to get state ferry service and decided the time had come to get in on the act.*

And so began "the ferry years"—the latest chapter in a long struggle to balance remoteness and accessibility. For a few charmed years islanders reveled in the convenient, easy access to the mainland. But the same stroke that delivered Swans Island to the doorstep of Middle America also delivered Middle America, in ever-increasing numbers, to the doorstep of Swans Island, and by the mid-1980s islanders found themselves caught up in a full-fledged development boom, with seasonal housing starts the highest in Hancock County. This, in turn, has sparked an energetic initiative by Swans Islanders to strengthen the year-round fishing economy as a hedge against unchecked summer development. In 1984 Swans Island lobstermen took the lead in establishing the state's first trap limit as a six-year pilot conservation project. And in 1989 Swans became the first community west of Passamaquoddy Bay to embrace salmon aquaculture as an economic alternative to seasonal recreational development.

Today, with 348 year-round residents, the community is neither as large nor as small as it has been, but it has managed to strike a stable balance between competing economic needs and use patterns and bustles with a sense of purposeful activity. After more than two centuries of surviving yo-yo-like swings of famine and fortune, islanders may have developed some fairly reliable survival instincts.

to summer vacationers. The work ethic of the islanders and their desire for independence seem well established. Population pressures are less likely to impair their quality of life than that of urbanites. But the pressures are there.

What's happening on Swans Island is the kind of a thing that has changed the character of North Haven, Vinalhaven, Islesboro, and other large Maine islands. Swans Island had 1,000 people at the beginning of this century. It has only 350 or so permanent residents today. It's going to gradually get more and more summer residents. I don't think there's any way anyone can stop that from happening because, among other things, there's a state ferry which will keep getting larger. At the beginning of the century, there was a large year-round population on Swans because of a quarry there that provided employment for a large number of islanders. But aside from lobstering and perhaps salmon aquaculture, it is not clear what can sustain people on Swans economically into the twenty-first century. So islanders will, I'm afraid, continue to sell to people from away.

The same thing is true of a good many other islands, such as Crotch Island and Stonington (which of course is no longer even an island). Crotch Island still operates occasionally to cut stone, mostly on a custom basis. Hall's Quarry on Mount Desert Island operates occasionally, but also on a custom basis. Orono Island is a fifty-acre island which I look at across the narrows from our house on Garden Point. There was once a railroad on Orono, part of the quarry operation which ran about ten years there. It is a rather high island surrounded by deep water. They quarried large blocks of granite and rolled them downhill on the railroad that was about two hundred yards long to load on the schooners waiting at the dock. When Orono was abandoned,

Charlie Rowe's tuna.

Handlining on Swans Island's once productive inshore cod grounds.

the island wasn't worth anything. Now the primary value of this island is as a summer place.

As the value of the Maine coast and islands increases for summertime uses, there will be pressures not just for larger ferries, but also for wider and better roads to bring in more people. I have seen the age of the automobile arrive in Maine, mostly from an offshore perspective as bridges were built, linking remote places to the mainland. When I first started coming to the Maine coast, the roads were so poor, there were only steamers serving most coastal locations. If there were bridges, they were designed to be drawbridges. Then, starting with the bridge to Deer Isle in 1939, the state began constructing modern bridges to many of the inshore islands. Most of the bridges were high enough to allow steamers to pass under them. But most of them were not high enough for masted vessels. The one over the Eggemoggin Reach to Deer Isle is eighty-odd feet above the water so large sailing vessels can't go under it. *Avelinda*, which had a mast seventy-one feet above the water, went under, but it was difficult as you approached to see whether there was sufficient clearance.

I've also watched as bridges were built to Beal's Island across Moosabec Reach off Jonesport, which is only thirty-odd feet above the low water. The bridge across the Lubec Narrows between Campobello Island and West Quoddy Head is another example. The bridge across the Sasanoa River, which cuts across the passage connecting Bath and Boothbay, is only fifty-five feet above high water. At the bridge at Wiscasset, you can only get a motorboat through that passage. All of these bridges are useful, but they bring many more tourists in than they carry Maine products out to the rest of the

Children of the cove.

world. Like everywhere else, the whole coast of the Gulf of Maine has been changed by the automobile. The automobile takes priority over anything that's sailing.

Those not born in Maine are identifiable as "from away," even after a lifetime in the state, and are never entirely accepted by those who were born there. The separation of people from away—summerfolk from year-round residents—is not a form of snobbery; it is more that the native fishermen and farmers and shopkeepers want to preserve their independence and not become cooks, caretakers, or choremen for people they didn't grow up with. Visitors who fail to understand this will not get a full measure of enjoyment from their visit to Maine.

Any avid sailor to Maine can tell why the coast is so attractive to cruisers. The challenge of the weather and the rocky shores, the variety provided by the ebb and flow of the tides, the beauty of the unspoiled islands, the sense of timelessness, the independence and self-reliance of the Maine people, their wit and good humor and peculiar idiom and accent—all these help, of course, but foremost is the evidence of hardships conquered and dangers averted, evidence of a people's heroism. That's what the Maine coast is all about.

There are other skippers of many years' experience who have no such tales to tell. If your enjoyment of cruising comes from showing a fine yacht to other sailors, or from sailing only between yacht clubs along well-traveled and buoyed passages, or from riding in the cockpit while professionals operate the yacht in familiar waters, it is easy to avoid a real encounter with this remarkable coast and its even more remarkable people. Our interest has been in ex-

Hockamock Head and Light at entrance to Burnt Cove Harbor.

ploring the inlets and meeting those who live and work by the sea and in seeing that some of the primeval beauty of this spectacular coast is saved for future generations. If someone has a good idea, I try to help. With regard to my philanthropic activities, my gray hairs and reputation have stood fairly well unimpaired and now many good organizations are carrying on the work of protecting the heritage we've been given.